HOW TO PLAY IN THE WOODS

ROBIN BLANKENSHIP

GIBBS SMITH
TO ENRICH AND INSPIRE HUMANKIND

First Edition
20 19 18 17 16   5 4 3 2 1

DISCLAIMER: Some of the activities suggested in this book require adult assistance and supervision. Children and their parents or guardians should always use common sense and good judgment in playing, cooking, and making crafts. The publisher and author assume no responsibility for any damages or injuries incurred while performing any of the activities in this book; neither are they responsible for the results of these recipes or projects.

Published by

Gibbs Smith

P.O. Box 667

Layton, Utah 84041

1.800.835.4993 orders

www.gibbs-smith.com

Designed by Nate Padavick

Printed and bound in China

Gibbs Smith books are printed on either recycled, 100% post-consumer waste, FSC-certified papers or on paper produced from sustainable PEFC-certified forest/controlled wood source. Learn more at www.pefc.org.

Library of Congress Cataloging-in-Publication Data
Names: Blankenship, Robin, 1959-
Title: How to play in the woods / Robin Blankenship.
Description: First Edition. | Salt Lake City : Gibbs Smith, [2016]
Identifiers: LCCN 2015032683 | ISBN 9781423641537
Subjects: LCSH: Outdoor life--Handbooks, manuals, etc. | Outdoor
   recreation--Handbooks, manuals, etc. | Wilderness survival--Handbooks,
   manuals, etc. | Camping--Handbooks, manuals, etc.
Classification: LCC GV191.6 .B54 2016 | DDC 796.5--dc23
LC record available at http://lccn.loc.gov/2015032683
ISBN 13: 978-1-4236-4153-7

CONTENTS

Stories at Rabbit Stick.

1991 MEL MANTHE

This book is written with gratitude, in memory of Melvin Manthey, who first taught me how to play in the woods.

Uncle Mel taught many children how to see the woods as a home. With a tattered-tail old crow named Charlie on his shoulder and an ornately carved and painted walking stick in hand, he would lead us through the woods to hunt for arrowheads and pottery shards, find wild onions and acorns, and see the hidden fox den and the thrush's invisible nest. He taught us to carve into wood the wonders we discovered, creating totem poles and great log drums. Under his care, we stayed out late at night, learning the names of the stars and the music of the barn owl.

He was not only a naturalist and artist, but also a writer. He made up epic stories, written in rhyme and meter in the style of Longfellow, of the history of the native people and the early pioneers in the Great Lakes area. Sitting on a mossy stump under an old spreading oak tree, he would read each newly written chapter of his tome, *The Honey Bee Tree.*

His stories, his artwork, his natural relationship with nature, and his selfless mentoring were the magic of my childhood.

INTRODUCTION

Greetings happy, expectant readers ready for a good romp and some fun learning in the woods. Here you will find activities and ideas that help make time spent in the woods more interactive with nature, that encourage us to immerse ourselves in the outdoors more often, that remind us of the satisfaction we feel when we are capable, competent, healthy, and free from prescribed schedules and "rules of play," and that help us remember, and relearn, the wisdom and ways of our ancestors in nature. These life ways have kept us alive, healthy, and fulfilled all these many years.

This "knowing" our ancient ancestors have passed to us, is alive in us—in ways our modern sciences are just starting to investigate—and ready to be remembered. Let the laboratories dig and dive, deciphering the data. Let the metaphysicians postulate and ponder, proffering philosophies.

Our job is to simply go play in the woods.

This said, I will address the current science, and sometimes share philosophical musings in these pages. If the referenced facts remind us why it is important to be in nature, and the musings stimulate a desire to cultivate deeper relationship with our natural world, good news. If, however, we are simply after the meaty facts that allow us to build a big bag of tricks for outdoor living and playing in the woods, more than enough will be found in these pages. Read it and stay focused on the goal of playing in the woods.

Activity descriptions in this book are preceded by ♦ one, ♦♦ two, or ♦♦♦ three arrowhead icons. If you are working with youth or wanting a progression of skills to work on yourself, from accessible and simple to more complex, you can begin by choosing a single arrowhead activity—the more difficult the activity, the more arrowhead icons.

Joy, health, and confidence to you!

Robin Blankenship

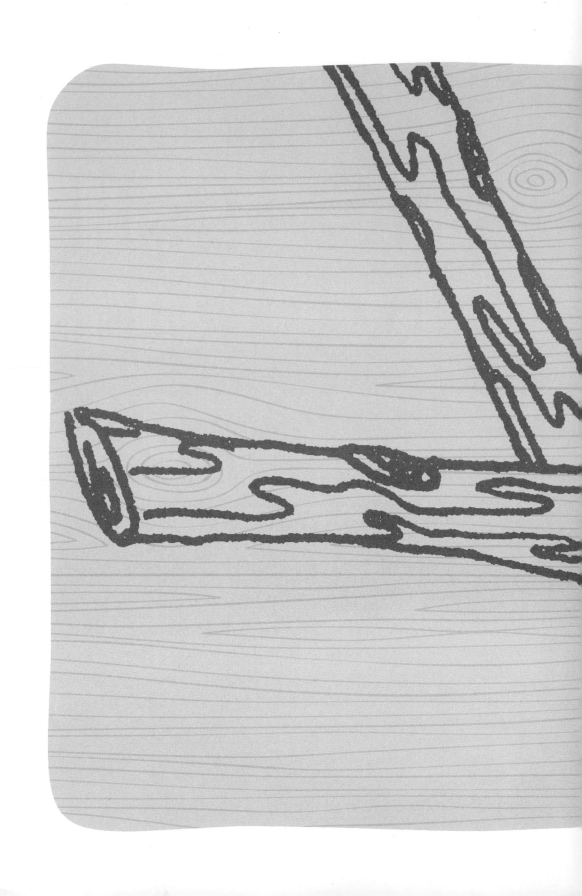

MAKE MUSIC WITH STICKS AND STONES

Have you ever picked up a stick and run it along a neighborhood fence line? A stick on a wooden fence makes a wonderful clack-itty-clack-clack-clack. Clack-itty-clack-clack-clack. A stick on chain link is stereo, reverberation.

IDEA

In the beginning, there was music: the crash of a wave, roar of thunder, rustle of a leaf, the dribble, dribble, drop, drop, pitter, patter, plop, splitter, splatter, splash of a drizzle turning to a drenching. Somewhere at the front of the human timeline, your ancestor leaned down, picked up a stone or a stick, and played along to the rhythms of nature.

Do you think you're musical? Have you ever had a music lesson? Outside, the lessons are free, the instruments are abundant, and the teacher persistent and patient. Scheduling, focus, and diligent practice are not required.

SIMPLE PERCUSSION BEAT WITH STICKS AND STONES

Head outside, pick up a stone or a stick, and start your own jam. Clap your hands, tap your stones, clack your sticks, and become a member of the longest-running musical performance group ever.

You'll be surprised once you start a stick-and-stone music session how many folks pop up to join you. The bigger surprise is how nature responds! Try it.

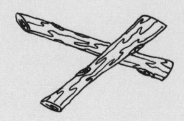

DESIGN YOUR MUSICAL STICKS

Now that you're a musician, why not decorate those sticks and stones? Imagine walking around with a pair of matched, beautifully designed music sticks. They are right there in your back pocket any time you feel inspired to play. Sharpies or colored markers work well for designing, or simply dipping the ends of your sticks in colorful paints can be beautiful. Painting your musical rocks or putting fun designs around their edges with a marker somehow makes them feel more like instruments, and you'll find yourself picking them up more often.

You can carve designs into your musical sticks, too, by using the edges of sharp rocks. Sharp rocks are great for carving in wood, but round smooth rocks make instruments that are easier to hold.

THROWING STICKS AND BOOMERANGS

Have you ever picked up a stick and just thrown it at something? Of course you have!

It seems like the older we get, the less we pick up a stick, and certainly, the less we throw it at something. Perhaps because when we pick up a stick these days, and throw it at something, there is no practical application.

IDEA

Our ancestors probably picked up a stick and threw it at something almost every day, and when they did, their efforts were well rewarded. This, of course, encouraged the activity, and so they became quite skillful at hitting whatever they threw a stick at, thus collecting food and resources on a daily basis.

It sounds simple, doesn't it?

THROWING STICKS TO HUNT SMALL GAME

So go ahead and pick up a stick. Throw it at something. Now, try to throw it at something as small as a squirrel. Go ahead, try again. Keep practicing. Pretty soon you'll be hitting that small of a target consistently. Like most things, it just takes practice.

KNOWLEDGE

Take some time to play around with different kinds of sticks. Hardwood (such as oak and hickory), green (live) wood, or sticks with lots of resin, all of which are heavier than dried-out sticks, fly through the air more quickly, and deliver more bang for their buck when they hit the target. After a while, you'll begin to notice that sticks of a certain shape fly through the air in a more controlled way and allow you to hit the target more often. That's good news!

If you practice throwing the stick as if you're trying to skip a stone on the pond instead of throwing it overhand, you'll have better aim. Now choose a stick with a slight bend. It will fly through the air with a controlled, horizontal spinning motion (think boomerang). If you flatten one side of the stick slightly and hold that flattened bottom toward the ground when you throw, the stick will maintain a more level flight trajectory. Now, if the bend in that stick is not right in the middle, but rather farther away from the end you're holding in your hand than it is from the end pointing out in the air, the flight pattern will be even more predictable.

IDEA

Make no mistake. Your ancestors really thought this through. After all, their lives depended on accuracy. And remember, even though they were ancestral people, ancient, primitive, cavemen, or any of the other names we know them by, they were in no way unintelligent. The thought process required to craft an excellent, accurate throwing stick is still used today in the creation of a jet airplane wing. That's high-tech thinking! Your ancestors were thinking at this high level and applying their intelligence to the materials at hand to provide for their daily needs, to create their art, to build their culture, and to ensure their survival. You come from a great and powerful people. We all do. Otherwise, we wouldn't be around today to talk about them. Think about that for a while.

As for the boomerang, a kind of throwing stick that actually returns to you and has been used on the planet for eons, think about the level of intelligence it takes to design that kind of flight pattern. Of course, if it's food we are after, we don't want our stick to return to us. But how convenient is it if we miss and find the stick right back in our own hand? It's a game of throw and return without the dog.

It's not too hard to imagine the possibility that a return-to-me throwing stick was crafted by one of our ancestors, not for a practical matter, but rather as a happy, playful, creative outlet. Why not? Ancestral people who had moved beyond subsistence hunting and gathering, whose bellies were full, and so perhaps had the time and energy to do more than think about acquiring and consuming food, are the ones who developed and left behind traces of rich cultures.

MAKE STRING AND ROPE FROM PLANT FIBERS

String, rope, fishing line, and lashing can be made from many kinds of plants and the barks of various bushes and trees. Whole leaves of certain plants, like cattail, can be twisted into rope and strong cord. When you know this, and know how to make plant materials into string or rope, there are so many outdoor living applications. It is useful knowledge for the survivalist.

QUESTION

Will this bark work? Will that leaf twist without breaking? Can I swing from a limb on this rope I made?

IDEA

When we walk into the woods asking good questions, we wake up a healthy imagination to new possibilities. This is so much more fun than walking into the woods with all the answers.

If you want to try these activities at home first, just use some strips of paper towel, or even some yarn or ribbon you have around the house. You might use your shoelaces or even your hair, if it is long enough, to get the idea.

TWISTING PLANT FIBER INTO STRING

If you're ready to head right out, grab up some tall grass and get started. If you take a single strand of grass and pull on it hard at each end, it is likely to break. But when you put several together and try pulling again, it is much stronger. Give it a try.

MAKE SOME STRING

Take several blades of tall green grass, and holding them in a bundle, twist them together along their length. Green grass works better than dry grass because it doesn't break as easily when you twist it. Dry grass will work too, but you'll want to get it wet first and twist it more gently. You have now given your blades of grass a **single spin**, in just the way that many yarns are made from animal fibers. You could simply wrap this around something you want to hold together and tie the ends in a knot.

For a stronger string or rope, you want to learn to twist the different strands of fiber around each other in a way that they will hold together. This is what rope makers call a **plied cord**. It means two or more simple spun fibers are then wrapped back around each other in the opposite direction they were spun the first time. Let's try it.

TWISTING PLANT FIBER INTO 2-PLY STRING

Hold about three lengths of grass that you have simply spun together, firmly between your thumbs and pointer fingers of each hand, with your fingers spaced about 1 inch apart, right in the middle of their length. The spun ends will unravel a little bit. Don't worry.

With the right thumb and pointer finger, twist gently away from you, while at the same time, with the left thumb and pointer finger, twist gently toward you. As you do this, a small loop will form in the center of the grass strands. Pinch this little loop tightly between your left thumb and finger, holding it in

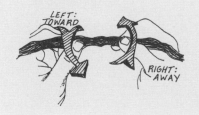

LEFT: TOWARD

RIGHT: AWAY

A SMALL LOOP WILL KINK IN THE CENTER

place, and letting the ends of the strands of grass fall over and down to the right of the small loop.

TAKE LOOP IN LEFT THUMB AND FINGER

Now take the strands that you twisted with your right fingers, the ones that are in the back of the little loop you made, and twist them gently away from you. When they are gently twisted away, bring them forward, toward you, and lay

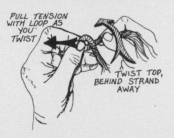

PULL TENSION WITH LOOP AS YOU TWIST

TWIST TOP, BEHIND STRAND AWAY

them in front, and a little below, the other strands of grass. Now take the other strands and twist those gently away from you. Once they are gently twisted away, lay them over the first set of strands. Take those first strands you twisted, twist them away again, and lay them over the other strands.

Keep going like this, slowly moving the pinch of your fingers along

LAY THE TWISTED STRAND IN FRONT AND BELOW THE UNTWISTED STRAND

where the cord is forming, so you can hold the grass strands securely as you twist them with the other hand. Moving the pinch along as you twist the two groups of grass strands is the best way to make a neat consistent twist in the grass.

The pinch of your left fingers is not holding the cord you are making together. It is the way you are twisting the grass and then laying it back over itself in the opposite direction that is actually allowing your string or rope to hold itself together. That means you can let go of it, even if it isn't finished, and go find more grass, or, go do anything else you want to do. If you do want to keep making your rope longer, simply add more strands of grass to each side whenever they are needed.

QUESTION

What's the difference between string and rope? Rope is fatter. How do you get fat string? Add more strands of grass when you start and as you add in pieces. If you're going to make something to swing on, it's good to have a fat rope.

KNOWLEDGE

Although more usually means stronger, it is also important how you twist the strands. If you give the same amount of twist to each side of strands in the rope-making process, you will allow the final rope to be stronger. This is true because when your weight hangs on the rope, it is equally absorbed by each twist in the same way.

This little bit of physics simply means that all along your rope, the same work-load is being asked of all strands. If you have areas that are twisted more tightly than the area right next to them, or in other parts of the rope further away, then the pull on that part of the rope when you hang on it creates more tension and makes it easier for your rope to break.

The amount of strands on each side of your rope as you make it is also important. Again, if the rope is about the same thickness all the way along its length, then when you swing on it and it stretches to hold your weight, it does so evenly and equally all the way up and down. So if you can twist consistently as you make the rope and keep the thickness of the rope equal, you will have a much stronger rope. Good news, especially if you plan to swing on it!

IDEA

Imagine for a moment other ways you might want to use rope or string out in the woods. If you like fishing in little creeks, you can easily find plants that have fiber to make good, strong string that can be very thin for fishing line. The trick is finding a quality fiber material and keeping your twist and your thickness consistent. Then when your fish begins to pull back on your handmade fishing line, the line doesn't break in a place where it is thinner, or too tightly twisted. Good news if you're hungry for that fish!

KNOWLEDGE

Three plants, found worldwide, have been used by our ancestors for rope, string lashing, and line, and eventually cloth making: *dogbane, nettle, milkweed.*

All three of these plants have a strong, flexible, and very thin outer bark along their stalk. The bark fiber of these plants can be prepared in the same way. Dogbane and nettle fibers are particularly water resistant. Forming milkweed fiber into string is easier if you keep the fiber wet. When milkweed fiber is dry, it cracks and breaks easily.

Some other plant fiber materials for string: flax, black walnut, Osage orange, elm, basswood, willow, big-leaf sage, cliff rose, yucca, cattail, tule, iris leaves, palm fronds, corn husk, grasses, and the inner bark of a coconut husk.

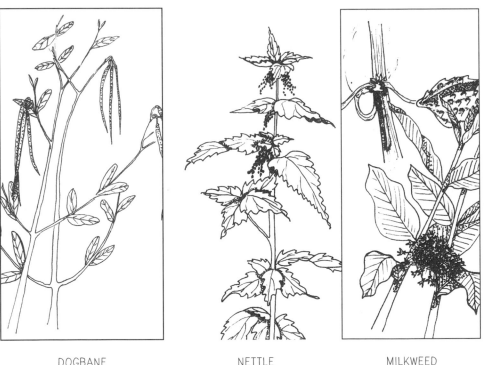

DOGBANE   NETTLE   MILKWEED

SPLITTING PLANT STALKS FOR STRING-MAKING MATERIAL

To prepare dogbane, nettle, and milkweed fibers, follow these simple directions:

Lay the plant stalk on a flat surface after you have removed any small branches off the top of the stalk.

Gently step on the stalk, with your foot set on it from heel to toe along its length, or firmly press down upon the stalk with the heel of your hand to flatten. Do this in a way that you do not break the stalk in small sections as it is flattened. The stalk will naturally split into four long quartered lengths as it is flattened. Practice this so you can split the lengths whole without breaking them into small pieces. This will make peeling the bark off the quarter splits much easier, and give you long lengths of fiber to make your rope and string.

KNOWLEDGE

When you have long lengths of fiber to work with, you add, or **splice in,** more fiber material less often, and your project moves along much more quickly. That said, it doesn't mean you should discard stalks that have broken along their length and not try to peel off the bark and use it in your project. Broken up quarters will create more work for you in the peeling, but they will give just as good quality fiber, because it is the inner hardened stalk that breaks, not the outer pliable fiber that you will use in your string or rope.

IMPORTANT

Any time you harvest a plant from nature for an activity, food on your table, or simply for its beauty, remember that nature's resources come in seasonal and limited supply. Harvest just what you need. Perhaps don't harvest anything if there isn't much available in that particular area and choose something else to do in the woods . . . like listen, or watch.

IDEA

You're out having fun in the woods. What you harvest is optional. The seed of the plant you *don't* harvest drops, grows again, and is an important part of the balance of nature. That plant affects the air and soil around it, supporting and interacting with other plants and microorganisms. Its importance in the environment is hard for us to remember, as most of us spend so little time in nature.

The animals, too, depend on plants for their very survival. All things are working together, at all times, all around us. Interdependence isn't just a vocabulary word you need to memorize for your biology test. *It is how life on Earth works.* Nothing stands alone. Relearning, respecting, and honoring this concept will make your time in the woods so much more fun and satisfying.

Just as the plants and animals need each other for life to be possible here on Earth, so are we a part of that great dance and balance, and our presence and activity in the woods, on the waters, and through the air is a blessing, a benefit, and a necessity to all life, measure for measure. Relearning this truth allows us to be joyful and effective as we interact in our natural world.

PEELING OUTER BARK FIBER OFF PLANT STALKS TO MAKE STRING

To peel the outer bark fiber off the stalk, hold one of the quartered lengths of the plant stalk in your hand that doesn't usually do all the work. (For me, it's my left hand.) Have the thick, or bottom end, upward and the inner stalk facing you, with the fibrous, flexible outer bark away from you, resting against your four fingers. Hold the stalk about 1 inch from the end. Hold it in place with your thumb pressing it against your four fingers.

Using the other hand, place the heel of your palm against the 1-inch stalk end that is sticking up. Now push back and away from you on that 1 inch of hard inner stalk until it breaks off. Grab the bottom of the piece of broken stalk and peel it up and away from you. Leave the outer fiber attached and unbroken. Let the hard inner piece drop to the ground. Now you have an inch of the flexible outer fibers sticking up above the hard inner stalk.

Leave your pointer finger right where the 1-inch piece of hard inner stalk broke off. This will help support the outer fiber as you grab the 1-inch outer fiber tassel and pull back, away from you and downward on the other side of your pointer finger, peeling that outer fiber off the inner stalk. ➡

KNOWLEDGE

As you peel the outer fiber down, the inner stalk will slowly rise, sliding gently up through the press of your thumb. Just peel about 2 inches of fiber down. If you try to pull more than this off at once, that outer fiber will taper off and break apart instead of staying in one long piece.

So now you have peeled back about 2 inches of the outer fiber and you have this piece of inner stalk sticking up above where you're pressing it between your thumb and pointer finger. Again, take the heel of your hand and press it against the sticking up part of the inner stalk, back away from you, to break off that inner stalk. Let it drop to the ground. Now you have a 3-inch, or so, tassel of fiber to grab hold of and pull and peel back and downward over your pointer finger again. Just peel about 2 more inches and then break off the inner stalk with your palm heel again.

Do this over and over until you have peeled the entire length of the stalk. Peel the other three quarters of stalk in the same way.

Since you now know that your string or rope won't unravel while you're making it, you can take these pieces of peeled fiber and start your fishing line, sewing thread, bow string, necklace, or rope swing right away. Then, just peel a new stalk and add that fiber to your started project. Or, you could peel all the fiber you want for your project first. This is the messy part of the project, and when you drop pieces of the inner stalk to the forest floor, you're simply helping nature by offering materials that will decompose to create more life-giving soil. No broom or dustpan required. Then you can take your peeled fiber inside and make your string and rope there if it gets dark.

IDEA

The fun part about making string or rope outside is the calming repetitive motion of your hands. As they peel and twist, these hand movements become easy, natural, and start to coordinate rhythmically with the sounds and motions of nature surrounding you. Once you are practiced and your hands move fluidly, the activity becomes calming and meditative, allowing your mind to relax and open up to creativity, and before you know it, you have a great big pile of fiber for your project. Now that's fun, healthy, and satisfying.

MAKE 2-PLY OR BRAIDED BRACELETS

CORD

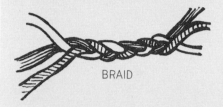

BRAID

SPIN

Making a corded bracelet out of plant fiber is easy and gives a unique look. The bracelet can be worn as a single loop, or a lot of length can be wrapped around multiple times. Try making several cords using different kinds of plants. This will give you a variety of colors, which you can then loop around your wrist or ankle in alternating patterns. Try braiding several colors together in a flat or round braid style for an intriguing bracelet. It's nature's bling!

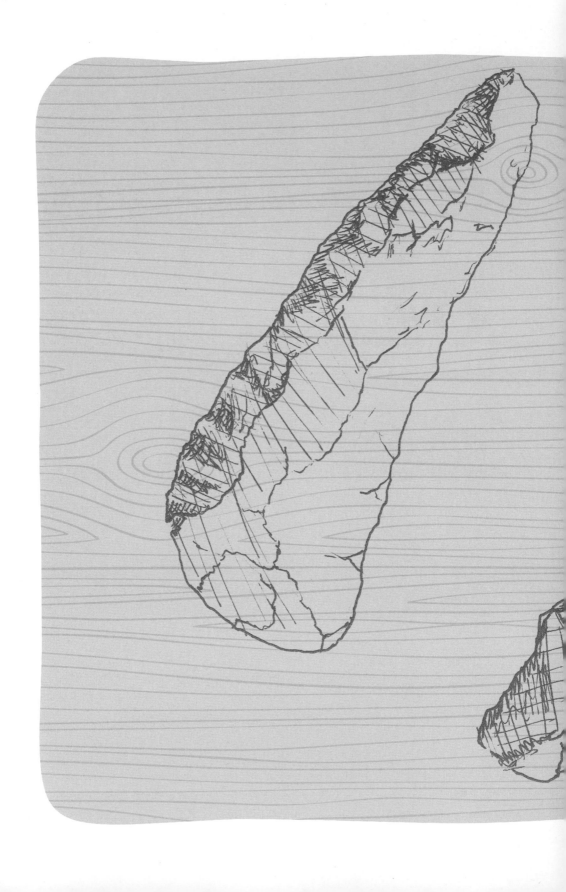

MAKE A
STONE KNIFE

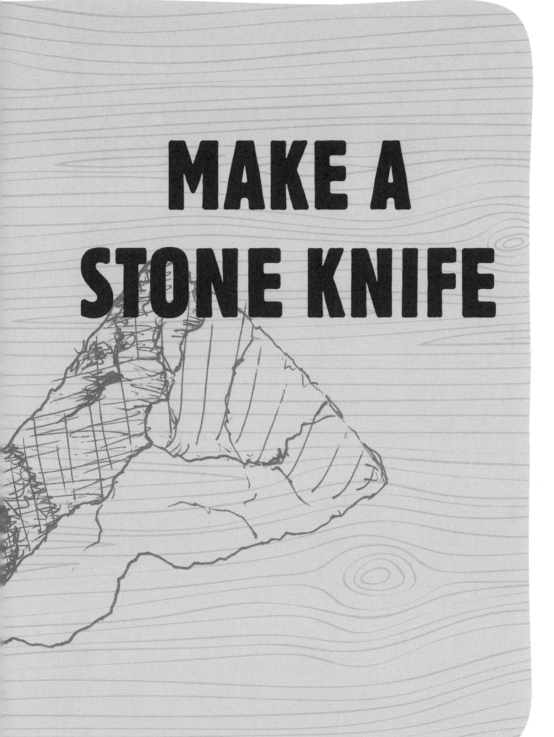

In almost all places, you can simply kick about for a while in the outdoors and find some kind of rock with a sharp edge. Different rocks make different kinds of edges, and some are sharper than others. Our ancestors probably used the rocks they found as tools long before they began to randomly break them and even longer before they began to break them in a premeditated manner to create particular shapes. This planned breaking and shaping of rocks is what we call **flint knapping**.

Most of the sharp rock edges you find in nature will work well enough to carve a point on a stick, to cut a stick in half, or to open up the belly of a fish you have caught on your handmade fishing line. There are, however, places where you can't even find a single stone or even a pebble. You can break a stick in half and use the jagged sharp edge of the break to clean your fish. Bones with sharp edges can be used for carving tools, but it always seems they are harder to find when you are really looking for them.

So let's just say you are in a place where there are stones, and you can't find any with the sharp edge to do the job you need to do. What now?

RANDOM ROCK BREAKING TO GET A SHARP-EDGED TOOL

Again following in the footsteps of our ancestors, take some stones and throw them on other stones so they shatter open and give lots of sharp-edged possibilities. You want to lift a fairly good-sized stone high above your head and throw it down with great force right onto the surface of another rock resting on the ground. This act of random breaking was probably the height of tool-making technology for a long period of human history. In the shards you find after breaking a rock this way, there will usually be one that will have a thin, sharp edge on one side, and a thick, less sharp edge on the opposite side. This makes it easy to hold the less sharp side in your hand, allowing you to apply pressure, and make a clean, controlled cut in the wood or cloth or meat that you want to cut with the sharper edge.

SAFETY

This random breaking sounds easy, hmm? Well, it also takes practice. To throw a heavy stone against another rock on the ground takes pretty good aim. You don't want to hit your toes while breaking rocks to make sharp stone knives. Be careful that little bits of rock don't fly up into your face or eyes when the rock breaks. It's a crazy, forceful, wild, random breaking after all, so bits and chunks and pieces can just go everywhere. It's a good thing if you have on some kind of glasses. Also, don't put sharp-edged rocks into your pockets. They will work their way through the cloth.

KNOWLEDGE

When a rock is smashed open, sometimes it breaks right in half or breaks into chunks that give us smaller-angled edges. This is good news if we want to make thin, sharp knife blades. Random breaking means you are randomly throwing the rock down and hoping for a good break. The way the rocks actually break is pretty consistent because of the way energy moves. Our ancestors noticed this pattern.

QUESTION

How did our ancestors move from random breaking to the predictable art of flint knapping?

CONSIDER

Our ancestors had an awareness of the world around them that we cannot even begin to understand. Even if you have wandered in the woods a lot, or spent many years traveling and living in the wilderness as I have, the level of observation and awareness we achieve as modern people does not come close to what our ancestors experienced. We are imprinted with our favorite songs that play most often on the radio and the funny commercials that come between them, what drama series might be on prime-time TV tonight, the sound of our nylon jacket and rubber shoe soles as we walk, the busy schedule waiting when we leave the woods, the brightly colored T-shirt we are wearing, the sound of an airplane overhead, and all the other possibilities that call our senses, thoughts, and memories to attention every waking moment.

IDEA
So imagine for a moment what a walk in the woods with your great, great, great, great, great, great, great, great, great . . . go about another 1,000 greats back after these first nine (that's a LONG time ago), and imagine that walk in the woods with your family. Every article of clothing was close to the color of the natural surroundings, probably made of animal skins or softened plant materials. No visual distraction. Paying attention and observing the details was a matter of life and death. If you didn't notice those plants over there, you might not be able to have a good dinner. If you didn't listen to the change in the birdsong, the running hooves of the deer, or the sudden, annoying chatter of a squirrel, you wouldn't be aware that a predator might be entering the area. Not paying attention? Maybe you would be the good dinner!

You were immersed in the natural environment on all sides, top and bottom. You watched the water flow, you watched the clouds shift and change, you saw the repetitive weather patterns come and go, and your constant observation and trained, focused awareness was not distracted, but rather enhanced, by the sights and sounds of the natural world around you. You had ability then to easily see the patterns of nature, the way energy moves in our world, through the water, through the air, and through the very mass of rock that had just broken apart at your feet when you threw it down to break into sharp edges.

KNOWLEDGE
Our ancestors could see the "track" that energy made through the rock once it was broken open. They knew energy moved in waves. They knew that energy moved out in all directions, not along a straight, flat line. They saw this in the water when a pebble broke the surface. They saw it in the cloud patterns formed by the wind. They saw this pattern, or track, in the broken stone, a track as clear and readable as the track of a raccoon in wet sand along the shoreline. They

didn't need a sixth-grade science book to describe the way energy works and to illustrate it on a two-dimensional page. They lived the way energy worked every day in a three-dimensional world. And they put this knowing to use in order to predictably break rock into useful tools. They knew:

Energy moves out in waves, with the first wave after impact being taller and less wide than the ones that follow (think of that pebble thrown into a pond or the wake of a boat).

Energy moves out in all directions from the point of origin (or in the case of stone knife making, from the point of impact).

The need to find a small angle on a chunk of rock to land a good hit so the energy could peel off a thin blade of stone was all the result of years of observation and immersion and excellent cognitive reasoning and problem solving.

CONSIDER

Our dirty, hairy, drag 'em-by-the-hair caveman ancestors were not nearly as backwards or brainless as we tend to think them. The human brain size has been relatively the same for a whole lot of years. It's a great big tool that has been well used for longer than we can imagine. Higher-concept thinking was not foreign to our ancestral family.

QUESTION

So, did you catch that? There are basically three things you need to know to make an excellent stone knife blade.

KNOWLEDGE

Energy moves out in waves. Energy moves out in all directions. Find a small angle on a chunk of rock to land a good hit. There it is! It really is that simple and will set you on the path to being an excellent stone-knife maker, opening up

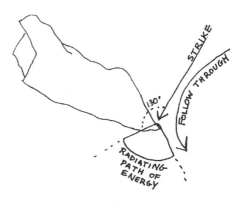

the invitation to explore the world of flint knapping for pleasure, creativity, art, and a fun thing to do while playing in the woods.

QUESTION
But wait! We're not finished. I am one of those people who always asks, "Why?"

IDEA
I want the long answer every time, because the long answer always leads to more questions, deeper learning, or knowing. That allows us to begin the journey of taking all that knowing, and synthesizing it into a life wisdom. Knowing things, having answers, is not the same as being wise. Still, I want to try to see around the corners and get the inside scoop. Then I begin to experience the truth that all things are connected, and this growing feeling of interconnection allows me to become a whole-concept thinker, and then there is no place my thoughts can go without spontaneously coming up with solutions. Solutions are not answers. They are *possibilities*. Operating from a platform of all possibilities leads to a life of wonder, richness, and deep participation. *Hmmm. All this from making a stone knife!*

PICK UP A ROCK TO IDENTIFY ANGLES FOR FLINT KNAPPING

So, pick up a chunk of rock with smallish angles on its surface.

Smallish angles mean angles around the exterior that are 90 degrees or less.

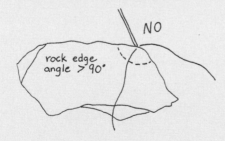

NO

rock edge angle > 90°

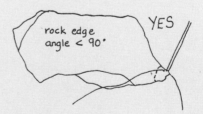

YES

rock edge angle < 90°

QUESTION

Why? Because you know that energy moves out in all directions. You also know you want to hit this rock with another stone in a way that allows it to break off a lovely, wicked-sharp peel of the outer shell to create a stone knife.

KNOWLEDGE

If you hit the original rock you want to make the knife from in the very center of its form and mass, where there are only angles larger than 90 degrees, the energy (force) of your strike will move out from the point of impact in all directions into the center of the mass of the rock. That means it will send all your striking effort into the full body of the rock. This results in a smashed impact area or, if you strike hard enough, the entire rock breaking apart into pieces. These pieces could be useful and serve as some kind of tool; however, I want to tell you how to get the ultimate, lovely, wicked-sharp knife blade.

QUESTION

Why? Because a sharp tool is much more safe. Because learning this is the first step in making a flint-knapped spearhead or arrowhead point. These blades can be your one-strike stone knife or be a blank for an arrow-head. Either way, it's a cool skill to know!

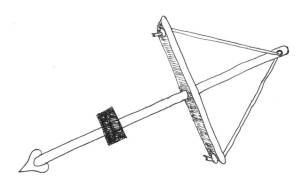

KNOWLEDGE

So you look for the angles that are *90 degrees or less*, and when you strike at them, you actually want to almost miss. That way, when you do impact the edge, almost all the energy of your strike goes out into thin air! This leaves just enough energy traveling along (in its wave pattern) to move through the outer shell of the mass of the rock and peel off that lovely, wicked-thin stone knife (or arrowhead blank).

Although energy does move out in all directions, it helps to visualize the energy moving out and downward, in the shape of a megaphone or a cone, from the point of impact. It also helps if you keep the rock you're striking tipped downward slightly as you strike it, and imagine that you're trying to send the energy out in a cone shape that expands out almost completely into thin air to the side of the rock edge, except one little peel of the edge of the side of that cone that is slicing down through the rock body before going out the bottom.

QUESTION

Can you imagine that? If not, keep trying. It is going to help you immensely.

Flint Knapping 101

MAKE A KNIFE BLANK: PART 1

So let's strike off a blade! Hold the rock with your hand that doesn't usually do all the work. Locate an edge that has an angle of 90 degrees or less. Hold the rock so that angle is opposite the grip of your hand, the stone is centered out in front of your stomach in mid-air, and one side of the angle is facing directly up to your eyes. The opposite side of the angle is facing the ground. You are going to strike along the angle edge facing you. Remember, you are going to almost miss. Keep the edge tipped downward.

Pick up another rock from the ground. Any rock will do, but it is better if it is rather rounded and rough, has a good weight to it, and it's not the exact same kind of rock you are trying to break.

QUESTION

Why? Often when you break a rock, striking at it with another rock of the exact same kind, the energy release at impact shoots into both pieces of rock at once, breaking both of them apart. (Remember, energy moves out in all directions.) It's better if the rock you are using to strike with has higher density, and is even a little porous, so it can both withstand and absorb the force of impact. We're getting a little picky here, but I'm guessing you want to get pretty good at this, and it never hurts to get the long answer.

KNOWLEDGE

Hopefully you picked up a rock that you want to break that isn't crumbly and full of cracks, crystals, or fossils. Usually these kinds of rocks don't break clean and strong, giving you a nice knife blade. But if that is all that's around, give it a try. Sometimes you're lucky. Luck is one thing. Now let's develop some skill.

♠♠ MAKE A KNIFE BLANK: PART 2

You're holding the rock you want to break in the right position, already described. You have the other rock you want to strike with in the opposite hand and you are holding it so that when you strike with it, you won't smash your fingers on the edge of the angle you are hitting. The way you are holding this striking rock would be rather like hammering with a short hammer that had a very fat handle. As you strike the angle edge, follow through with the arc of your strike. Swing down and past the edge. It is very important to allow the arc of your strike to

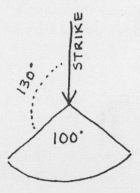

follow through completely once the edge has been struck. If you play or practice any kind of sports that require using a racket or bat, you already understand how important follow-through is for success. This will take some practice.

KNOWLEDGE

After the impact of your strike, as you are following through the full arc of your swing, it is easy to catch your pointer finger knuckles on the edge you are striking. Keep this in mind as you strike the rock you want to break.

♠♠ MAKE A KNIFE BLANK: PART 3

All right. Get busy. Strike, strike, and strike again. Imagine the cone pattern of the outgoing energy is radiating out mostly into the air off to the side of the rock you are striking. Remember, you are almost missing that edge. Sometimes you miss it several times in a row and you feel pretty foolish. Thank goodness you're out in the woods having fun and being silly. Just smile as you miss and know you're doing everything right.

KNOWLEDGE

As your hand-eye coordination improves and you begin to strike the edge consistently, you'll want to remember that energy moves in waves. If you strike right at the very edge, that first wave pattern in the rock, the one where the wave is very high and close to the next one, won't have enough width to move down through the rock and peel off the perfect blade. Rather, the wave pattern will start to form as the energy moves into the rock, and then just roll out into thin air, leaving you a very short piece of sharp stone to work with. You can certainly do something with it, but keep practicing until you hit it in just the right spot, just a little back from the edge, so a nice blade of stone can peel off, and you can run your finger along the beautiful wavy track energy has made through your stone.

CONSIDER

Think how many times your ancestors must have traced their finger in just the same way down a beautiful, fresh blade of rock, exposing to the light, air, and eye the core of what had been hidden for many years.

Stone Tools by Grinding

OF INTEREST

You just learned how to get a sharp stone knife tool by random breaking or by applying the basic first steps of flint knapping. Without knowing the basics of fracture mechanics, you can still make all kinds of stone tools by grinding. Many stone artifacts are found that were made by grinding. Some of the most remarkable ancient stone axe and adze tools were all made by grinding and shaping, not flint knapping.

Larry Kinsella has done a lot of research and spent a lot of time re-creating some of these tools. He makes many replicas of ground stone axes that a modern-day strongman can hardly wield. He also happens to be an incredible flint knapper, an enthusiastic and astute historian, and does a lot of great educational work at the Cahokia Mounds World Historic site. His real claim to fame, though, is being married to an awesome storyteller, Marilyn (more about her in Tricks and Tips for Telling a Good Story, p. 75).

HISTORY

Cahokia Mounds is an area between Missouri and Illinois, near St. Louis, where people lived many thousands of years ago in a complex society, leaving behind a stunning array of architecture and artifacts that tell the story of their daily lives. Many of these impressive stone tools can be seen there. If you get a chance to go to Cahokia, make it happen. This civilization is on par with anything found in the history of the Aztec.

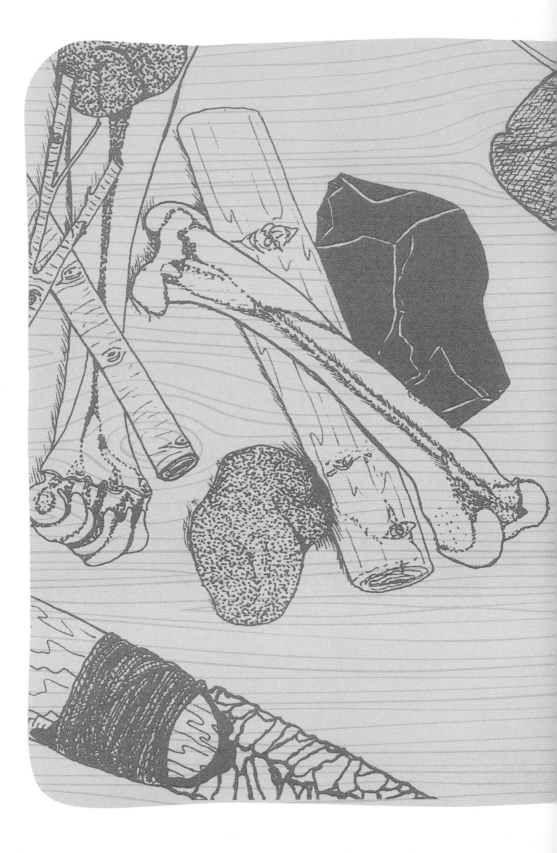

SAFE HANDLING OF TOOLS AND KNIVES

If we don't include a fork and table knife in a list of tools we regularly use, we hardly let children try using any kind of tool anymore, and many adults have little experience using tools on a daily basis. Even the innocuous silverware set can often be the cause of serious (and embarrassing) injury. We're pretty good at flipping switches, pushing buttons, and turning keys, however, none of these feats require close control, a steady hand, applied pressure, accurate movement, and/or a high level of safety awareness, so many of us have become unpracticed in the safe handling of tools.

We are making tools and using tools in all these activities, so it is good to start at the beginning and err on the side of assumption: little to no knowledge of tool use. Let's start from square one with safe tool handling.

There are very different ways of handling the many kinds of tools, and there is even a difference in the handling of a stone knife as compared to a steel knife. Tool-and-knife handling craftsmanship comes with experience. The more you work with your tools, or stone or steel knives, the more control and accuracy you will have in using them. Still, there are some basic principles that apply overall.

CONSIDER

Almost everyone will agree that a sharp tool should never be used in a way that the sharp edge comes toward the user. I have spent many years teaching knife safety and start with young ones by saying these words: Never carve toward yourself!

JUDGMENT AND SKILL, NOT RULES

Even so, skilled tool users (think chef or woodcarver) often use brilliantly sharp knives and bring them in a direction toward their hands and bodies as they use them. The control required to do this safely takes practice and time. And you can bet that most people who are expert tool users have a few scars to show for their days of practice and learning, or even for days they weren't focused and aware as they used their tool, regardless of their years of experience. So your level of **awareness and focus when using tools is most important.**

KNOWLEDGE

If a tool has a sharp edge, **keeping it sharp** helps you be safe.

QUESTION

Why? The sharp edge can do the work without you needing to apply a lot of pressure or force. Then, if you are not pushing very hard and the tool slips, you are less likely to get a serious injury. It is never a good plan to use your lap, leg, or hand to hold your project and push your sharp tool toward those body parts. Again, if the tool slips, you will have a cut or a puncture. If you are placing your project on a surface and applying pressure with your tool, make sure you understand where the tool will go if it slips off the project or you lose control of the tool.

CONSIDER

Make sure the tool you are using is the tool that will give you the result you want. Trying to make a tool do a job it isn't suited for (think using scissors to pry a paint can lid off) really ups your odds of breaking the tool, doing bodily injury, and/or ruining your project. Young children and adults of all ages can use a wide variety of tools in a safe manner. Like anything else, it's about practice.

If you made a stone knife already, you were using a rock as a hammer or striker, and perhaps you have a few marks on your fingers to tell the "I'm learning" story. Safe handling of a hammer stone means focus! It means concentrating on your grip enough not to drop the rock on your toe after impact. (Unfortunately, this is rather common, and you are laughing right now, or maybe you are crying, because you can relate!) It means **being super aware** of where your finger tips and knuckles are as you wield the hammer against sharp edges. **It means thinking about protecting your eyes!**

IMPORTANT

Hopefully you have followed the directions well enough to make a stone knife. Using it safely means never putting it in your pocket and walking around without wrapping it up in a piece of cloth, leather, or bark first. If you don't wrap it up first, it will cut right through your pocket and drop out or cut into your skin.

When you use it to cut something, hold it on the side that has the thickest, dullest edge. You can grind the holding edge on another rougher rock or even on the sidewalk. You can also hold the stone knife with a little pad of cloth or leather or even plant leaves to keep the edges from cutting into your hand when you apply pressure to cut.

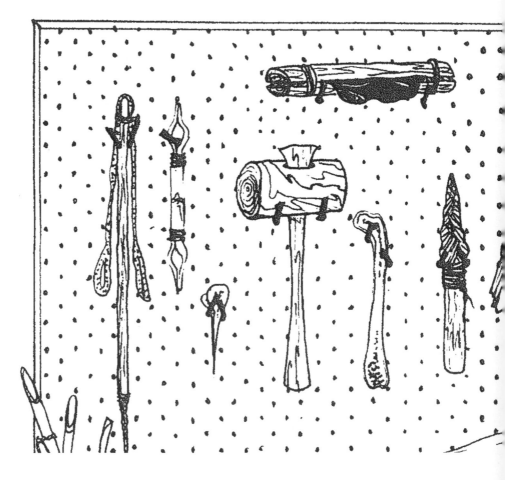

SAFETY

Don't use your stone knife while holding your project, or whatever it is you're trying to cut, against your leg, hand, stomach, or chest area. This sounds really obvious, but when you're in the middle of working on a project and you are calm and your mind is being open and creative, it's pretty easy to hold something up against yourself in a way that could be dangerous as you work to get your stone edge into just the right angle to remove or cut something exactly the way you want it. When using your stone knife, **discipline your thoughts and stay focused** on using your tool correctly and safely.

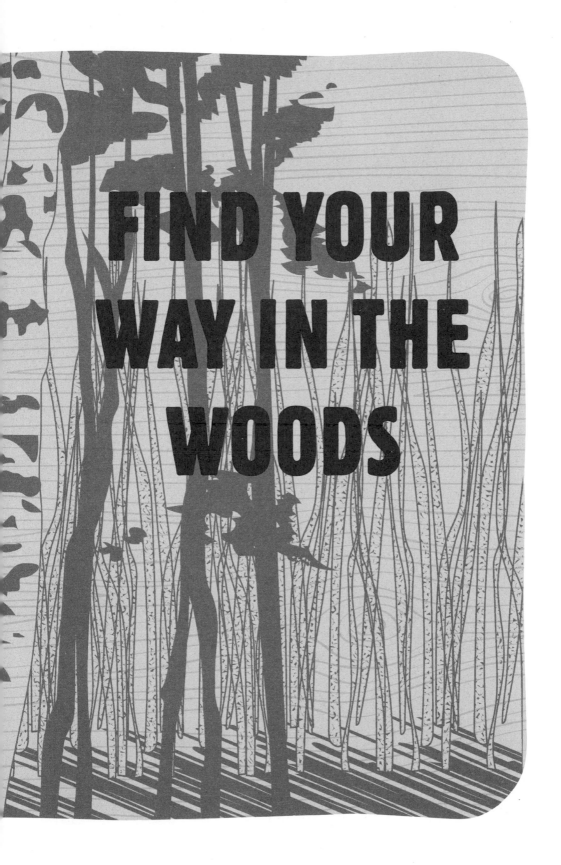

It seems like many adults and kids you talk to are really frightened of getting lost in the woods. This may be part of why people don't play in the woods as often as they might. When you consider the number of people who actually get lost in the woods, in comparison to the number of people who spend time out in the woods, it seems curious that we hold such a concern about getting lost and never being found.

Of course, when someone does get lost in the woods, the stories that get told are very dramatic and frightening. Even so, most whom are lost are eventually found, or find their own way home, thank goodness, and almost always the best parts of the stories are the difficult conditions they overcome, the strategies they use to overcome their fears, and the wondrous and amazing ways assistance is provided.

OBSERVATION

Survival programs and products stay in business training and equipping outdoor enthusiasts to overcome unforeseen accident or injury, prevent getting lost, or provide enough gear to survive being lost until found. This is good training. It's interesting, however, that many participants in these programs or purchasers of these products are motivated from a place of fear or discomfort.

QUESTION

What if you walked out into wild spaces and felt relaxed, joyful, and completely at home? This freedom is possible. Spending time in the woods, being immersed in natural environments, and giving yourself the opportunity to learn the lay of the land are all very effective means of overcoming unwarranted fears.

IDEA

We already gave some thought to what the world was like for our ancestors. We imagined the visual and audible input they might have experienced throughout their day, their keen observation of natural patterns, their broad awareness of shifts and changes in daily rhythms, their deep perception of interdependence. Now I suppose if you're being chased by a saber-toothed tiger or a cave bear, discomfort, distress, fear, and helplessness would be natural responses! But it isn't hard to believe that most days our ancestors walked about in the woods in comfort, joy, and feeling completely at home. After all, they were at home, and they knew their home turf as intimately as you know your living room.

CONSIDER

As for wayfinding, try for a moment longer to put yourself in the mindset of your ancestors. You are completely at home in the natural environment. You are fully aware of the cycles of weather, the change in moisture and wind direction, you see patterns of the way plants and trees grow and you instantly feel the difference in the air on your skin in moist areas compared to dry. You have a deep sense of place, and a direct relationship to the rocks, plants, and animals around you.

Your ancestors moved through the natural environment identifying, cataloging, and remembering the placement of foods and resources just as unconsciously as you now move through your neighborhood grocery store or supermarket aisles.

QUESTION

When you go shopping each week, do you harbor a fear of getting lost in the aisles and never returning home? It's hard for me to imagine that our ancestors had to work very hard at developing wayfinding skills. If you have spent an extended time in undeveloped areas, it is uncanny how quickly your sense of direction develops and how easy it is for you to predict the approximate time of day. You soak up the lay of the land in some unseen osmotic process, intuitively sensing how to get from whence you came. The shifting light as the day began, progresses and fades, silently keeping you tuned to the cycling of the moments. Those who have experienced this are nodding their heads right now.

IDEA

Innate wayfinding skills are a part of our human heritage, and just like learning to ride a bike and never really forgetting how, if you'll go out into the woods and make a point to spend some time there, your wayfinding skills find their own way onto the list of things you are relearning, remembering.

SUN SHADOW TRICK FOR DIRECTION

One way you can have fun playing in the woods and developing your awareness and wayfinding skills it by tracking the path of the sun. It is also a helpful trick if knowing the cardinal directions (**north, east, south, and west**) would be helpful to you in getting some-where you want to go (like home after a long day of wandering in the woods). I describe direction finding from a western hemisphere, North American perspective.

Set a tall stick straight up in an area where it will cast a shadow for several consecutive hours. Watch the shadow of the stick and note the way it moves over the land. Draw an arrow in the direction the shadow is moving. That arrow will point eastward.

QUESTION

Why? Because, as many of us are aware, our beautiful Earth is spinning around and around its center as it moves through the heavens. As it spins around its own center, making one full turn in an amount of moments we humans have cho-sen to call twenty-four hours, it is, at the very same time, making a big, circular (sort of) loop around the bright burning ball of gas we choose to call the sun, a star that makes life as we know it possible on Earth. Pretty cool stuff, huh?

KNOWLEDGE

This lovely little collection of whirling life is also spinning in a direction we choose to call counterclockwise, opposite the clockwise direction that the hands on clocks move, tracking the time it takes our planet to spin around each day and rotate each year around its sun.

From where we are standing on the surface of the earth, when we look out as far as we can see, to the place where our eyes see the land meet the sky, which we call a horizon, that spreads out all around us toward all cardinal directions, (**north, northwest, west, southwest, south, southeast, east, northeast**) we get the visual perception of the sun rising up from the horizon in the eastern sky, climbing up above us in the middle or brightest part of our day time, and setting in the western sky.

If you are trying to find your way, this alone is very good information.

Better still is realizing that your stick, and all the other tall things sticking straight up right off the surface of the earth, is casting a shadow throughout the day when the sun is shining on us. Because the sun's light is so bright and can penetrate a barrier of clouds surrounding our Earth, we can see shadows on lots of days that don't have direct sunlight or are somewhat cloudy and gray. So our shadow trick can still work even when the sun isn't shining brightly as long as there's a little bit of shadow to be seen on the ground.

The better part of all these things sticking straight up and casting shadows on the ground is that we always know first thing in the morning, if we can see the shadows, the shadows are stretching out in a westerly direction from the base of the object casting them. Throughout the morning hours, as the shadows get shorter and shorter, they are still forming on the ground in a westerly direction until noon, when the sun is pretty much directly overhead. As the morning gives way to afternoon, the shadows begin to lengthen again, on the opposite side of the object. They grow longer as the evening approaches, pointing in an easterly direction.

DRAW EAST, WEST, NORTH, AND SOUTH LINES USING SHADOWS

If you draw that arrow in the way the shadow is moving, it will be a line from **west** to **east** in the dirt. Using the shadows as a guide, all you need to do to know **north** and **south** is draw a line straight through and at right angles to your first line.

USE A STICK AND PEBBLE MARKERS

The stick and pebble trick works really well when there aren't a lot of tall objects to cast shadows in the area you are in. After you place the stick straight up in the ground, take a little pebble or a piece of bark and set it on the ground at the far end or tip of the shadow. Wait about 20 minutes and then take another pebble or piece of bark and set it where the end of the shadow now is. Don't move your first marker. Continue to place a marker at the far tip of the stick's shadow every 20 minutes or so. As you place the markers, a row will form from west to east. The row won't be exactly straight, because the earth isn't straight, but it will be close enough for you to determine east, west, north, and south.

AWARENESS ACTIVITY

Next time you run out in the woods to play, set up a stick and collect some markers. Once you have several markers in a row, you will know your east-west line. Look around and get a sense of the lay of the land in terms of the four cardinal directions. Pick out obvious visual landmarks and call out the direction in which they are.

Do this in many different places as you travel around your favorite areas of the woods. Pretty soon you'll have a good sense of which direction you're going no matter where you walk around. You'll start to feel more comfortable and relaxed and more at home when you go to play in the woods. It will also make other woods wanderers quite curious about the little line of stones they find with the sticks sticking up in the middle of them.

AWARENESS ACTIVITY

As you head out into the woods, pay attention to where the sun is on your body. If you leave in the morning and return before noon, getting back to where you started might then be as simple as keeping the sun on the opposite side of your body when you return. If you're going to be out all day long, you would have the sun shining on your body on the same side when you return.

Now of course this won't hold true if you are walking around in circles, but if you need to travel a ways in a somewhat straight line, this will help keep you from walking in circles as well. You have to think about these simple things at first, but after a while, they become more natural to you and you respond to nature's cues and find your way more intuitively.

NIGHT HIKE WITH MOON SHADOW

While the moon is out, you can use the stick trick with the moon's shadow and also the idea of being aware of what side of your body it is shining on. Go out for a night hike and try it out. The woods are magical at night. It is a time humans like to sleep, and we rarely get to experience the adventure of night. Try staying up now and then. It's worth it.

KNOWLEDGE

The moon is similar to the sun in that we perceive it to rise in the eastern sky and set in the west. Knowing this helps you determine cardinal directions at night, and when the moon is out, it is more difficult to see the stars that might help you find direction. Unlike the sun, the moon rises about an hour later each night as it grows full or **waxes,** rising later and later as it shrinks back to half and quarter, **wanes.** Because of this, we often get to see the moon in the daytime sky.

MAKE SHELTERS AND FORTS FOR FUN

Building shelters is fun. In all these years of teaching in the outdoors, I've never met anyone who didn't enjoy it. We have been seeking shelter from the first moments of human history, and the desire, willingness, and satisfaction of it are as natural to us as breathing. For now, let's look at shelter building from the perspective of playing in the woods. There are many practical and survival considerations about shelter discussed in Survival Shelters, p. 183.

QUESTION

Where will you build your shelter? Find a place that can be your special spot. You could go there to write or draw, listen to the sounds of the woods, or to nap. You could go there to hide for a few hours and see what wanders by or what animal adventures you might witness. Marvelous life stories are being performed all around you. In nature, the performances are free and you are always invited to be part of the audience. I have witnessed the most incredible dramas, comedies, mysteries, and miracles, all for the willingness to be present and to watch and sometimes to participate.

BUILD A STICK FRAME SHELTER: PART 1

A simple shelter framework can be made by laying a long pole-like stick that you find on the ground into the low notch of a tree. Then take more lengths of sticks and lean them up against one side of the pole at a good angle. They will rest where you set them and provide a wind break, shade, or just a comfy feeling of cover. This is fun to do in a little tucked-away place that you find yourself continuing to come back to. There is a sense of home-steading, moving into the nature neighborhood, and a sheltered spot to sit quietly and rest. Most of us find pleasure in it. It is a fun way to spend time in the woods.

BUILD A STICK FRAME SHELTER: PART 2

Once you have a basic framework, you can elaborate on your roof and wall designs. Are you just looking for a little shade, or are you looking for a hidden hollow? Are you wanting warmth and a wind break, or are you hoping to create a **blind** (a camouflaged cover that allows you to watch without being recognized as human) to observe wildlife? It is really fun to make your shelter look like a part of nature that passersby wouldn't even identify as something made by human hands.

When you get practiced at mimicking nature's patterns, even the animals become less timid and come very close, sometimes nibbling on parts of your shelter, sometimes stealing some of your building materials for their own! If you are inside, this is so much more of a thrill than any nature program on TV could ever be.

BONUS

The added benefit is that you begin to get a close-up view of how animals behave, what their patterns and habits and preferences are, and if you are interested in animal tracks, you can see what actions created the variations in the tracks you find. Sometimes you are so well naturalized that small animals and birds come right up, on, and over you. If you don't wiggle, flinch, or scream, which is really hard, it is a thrill much bigger than a roller-coaster ride.

MAKE A SAND MAT FOR TRACKING

You can find out what kind of critters have visited your secret spot while you were away. Put a small welcome mat of soft dirt or sand close by. Each time you return, you can check that area for tracks or disturbances. Sometimes you may come back to your shelter and find you have squatters!

GATHER WILD FOOD IN THE CITY

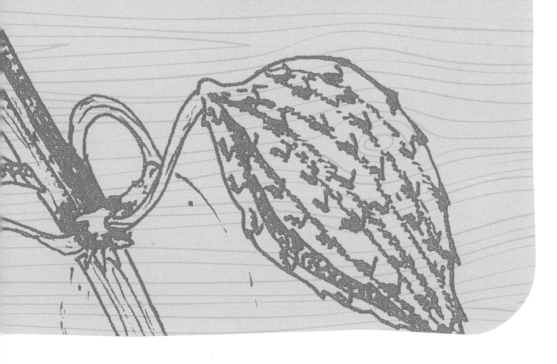

For most of our history, we humans have hunted for plant and animal foods. Scouring the banks of creeks and rivers, hillsides, woods, and plains, we searched out the areas where edible plants grew. We created weapons and tracked and trapped animals to kill for food. This hunter-gatherer existence developed us physically, emotionally, and spiritually. It determined the way we look and move and the way we mentally process and problem solve, and it formed a subconscious framework for how we perceive and interact with our world. How satisfying it is to stay involved in this ancient process, hunting down and identifying the foodstuffs that sustain us and make living possible.

HEADS UP

Let's start with where many of us live: urban and suburban areas. In the other food and cooking sections of this book—Gather Wild Food in the Forest, p. 269; Make Meals on the Campfire Coals, p. 201; and Dutch Oven Cooking, p. 279—we look at identifying food sources further afield and different ways of cooking outdoors. For now, however, let's look at what we can do right around our houses or apartments and in our own backyards.

Even if you live in the heart of an urban area, there are many kinds of bushes, trees, and flowers that provide delicious human fare. Learning to identify these food resources and putting them to use is a lot of fun. In flower boxes and planters across any city or town, there are many kinds of edible flowers and herbs: violets, nasturtiums, and mint, to name a few. Make sure you know these food sources haven't been treated with pesticides or fungicides before you harvest. Most backyards and planted public areas are not treated with toxins, but it is a good idea to make sure. All these free foods make beautiful and tasty additions to the food we already eat.

Many trees used for landscaping city parks and avenues provide bountiful and healthful foods and medicines—fruit and nut trees provide food, and linden or basswood trees (which are favored in American urban and suburban land-scaping) provide wonderful medicinal flower heads. There is an abundance of information available on the identification and use of flowering plants, woody shrubs, and trees, so it's easy to learn about what edible and medicinal natural resources are available for free all around us. (See Resources, p. 302.)

IDENTIFY EDIBLE PLANTS IN YOUR NEIGHBORHOOD

The next step then, after a little investigation of the medicinal and edible plant resources in your area, is to go out and identify these resources. Here is what I suggest: go to a local garden center or nursery and write down the names of the different plants you have seen in your neighborhood.

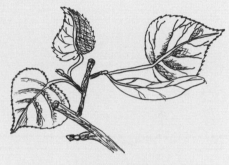

LINDEN TREE

If you've never even thought about plants before, or paid much attention at all to what is growing around your area, take a walk around the block first. Walk past the bank, the library, the city park, and the playground, and check the medians in your nearest shopping center. The very best apricot jam I ever made came from a dwarf apricot tree in the parking lot of a grocery store. Make a visual memory or a little sketch, or perhaps take a photograph, of what you see. Then go into a garden center or nursery and figure out what's out there. This is actually a whole heck of a lot of fun, and it's a great thing to do with friends.

You will notice right away that a lot of the plant life you encounter is not purposely landscaped or cultivated. Much of what you find will be wild flowers and plants or little renegade colonies of plant life that have escaped the confines of their planters or garden beds, their seeds carried to a new location by the wind or by hitchhiking along on passing animals and humans.

REFLECTION

There is a lonely little stretch of river in the wild where I love to paddle. A solitary peach tree spreads out and thrives along the bank. You would not find another peach tree for many hundreds of miles in any direction. Many years ago, some fishermen or boater, a bird, or maybe even just the river current itself dropped or carried that little seed to just the right place on the river bank. With just the right amount of nutrition in the soil, water, sunlight warmth, and shelter from the wind, a tree grew so that now, late in the summer, the branches hang heavy with beautiful, golden-orange, ripe, juicy peaches. I'm not sure if I'm more motivated to get down that river because of the paddle or the peaches! Anyway, you can't keep a good life down, so when you start to look, you will find plants everywhere, springing up in every urban nook and cranny and crack. Many of these we call weeds.

KNOWLEDGE

Even though many of the flowers, bushes, and trees we cultivate and encourage in developed areas are often useful for food and medicine, the weeds are usually even better. What a wonderful thing to know. Available for free when you know what to look for, your grocery and pharmacy options have just exponentially expanded, even when you live downtown!

HISTORY

Some of those weedy choices have been on the planet a very long time, like we have, and have helped determine the form and function of the very body we walk around in today. Your ancestors were searching for those very weeds and gathering them up as a staple food source and as helpful medicines. For a very long time, humans have been eating, and thriving on, many things we call weeds and currently try to eliminate from our homes, gardens, town streets, and agricultural fields.

KNOWLEDGE

Let's take it further. These wild weeds are some of the most nutritious plant food on Earth. They often contain more vitamins, minerals, and proteins (yes, I said proteins) than most of what you can buy in a modern grocery store. Wow!

GATHER WILD FOOD

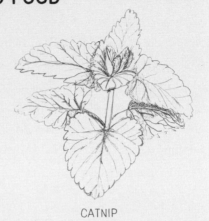

CATNIP

Now, if you will gather up a little bit of that wild food and add even the smallest amounts to your meals, you will feel the difference in energy, strength, and well-being. What a deal! It is as if your highly engineered machine (body) has finally gotten the high-octane fuel (food) it was designed to run on.

CONSIDER

The body you walk around in today was formed, and works like it does, because of the history of what your ancestors fed it and the environment in which they lived. Imagine that food and that environment. No wonder we're so beautiful! Any time you feed it what it was designed to digest (wild plant and animal foods), and put it in the environment in which it was formed to be most suited to (the outdoors), you are giving that body everything it needs to function at an optimal level. This isn't very hard to do, no matter where you live.

KNOWLEDGE

Like most life-forms we know, if we change our food and environment, our form will change and adapt to its new food and environment.

OBSERVATION

Recently in human history, many of us have chosen to create, eat, and offer to our young things like Twinkies and Minute Rice, and to drink a variety of liquids that do not have nutritional value to our bodies. This is a simple observation of, not a judgment about, the modern diet. If we continue this long enough, the human form will look very different from the way it does today.

CONSIDER

Remember, you're still walking around in a body that was grown by wild plant and animal foods, regardless of the current food choices you make—and you get to make any choices you want to. It just shouldn't be surprising, then, when you don't have a lot of energy, your mind doesn't focus and work well, you often feel ill or out of sorts, and many of your food choices leave your tummy feeling unsatisfied.

LAMBS QUARTER

GREAT NEWS!

Even adding just a little bit of the wild, weedy foods to the modern food you choose to eat already, whatever those choices are, will make a noticeable difference, in a relatively short order of time, to how well you feel each day. Over the last thirty-some years of teaching folks to use edible and medicinal wild plants, I've found that every person who tries this has experienced improved health and attitude, even if they only incorporate the smallest amount to their TV dinner or fast-food entrée.

REFLECTION

As for me, I am a bottom feeder! I have worked too many survival trips to turn my nose up at any kind of food. Anything that can't run away from me is fair game—literally. I am not picky, and I am not a purist. That said, many times during the day—whether I'm out playing in the woods, hanging out close to home, or visiting friends in an urban environment—I am usually leaning down periodically and grazing from the smorgasbord of wild plants that is constantly available. Perhaps I take in a meager half cup of wild plant foods most days, sometimes less. Because of the work I have done all these years and the lifestyle I've chosen, I eat more like our ancestors than most people I know.

MORE GREAT NEWS!

I am telling you here that even if you don't really make good food choices at all, you will benefit by becoming a modern grazer, without changing any of your other choices. How lovely! And it is fun and free! Like I said earlier, what a deal!

KNOWLEDGE

If you live in rural environments surrounding urban areas, you have even more access to free plant and animal food: the roadsides of America are a veritable feast.

INFORMATION

Some of my favorite books for beginning to identify plants around the outskirts of town and out in the countryside, along the hedges and creeks and over hill and dale, are those of the author Euell Gibbons. He shared the knowledge of wild edible plants through his books and film shows, and he became pretty well known nationwide for endorsing a certain kind of healthy cereal on TV when I was a kid. His books are a valuable resource, and the great thing about plant knowledge is that it's not very likely to go out of date anytime soon. A good plant book is a good plant book.

Several more recent edible and medicinal plant authors that I recommend are: John Mioncynzski, Cattail Bob Seebeck, Susun Weed, Samuel Thayer and Rosemary Gladstar, Doug Elliot, Ben Charles Harris, and David Arora. (See Resources, p. 302.)

KNOWLEDGE

In almost all environments across North America, you can find five plants that I consider to be the most important to learn to identify. Knowing these five will mean you always have food: **lamb's quarter**, **purslane**, **amaranth**, **nettle**, and **dandelion**.

PURSLANE

Hmmm . . . these are all plants that we consider weeds, but they offer more nutrition, vitamins, and minerals than the produce we eat from the grocery store! All of them can be eaten raw, and amaranth, nettle, and lamb's quarter produce seed that is very high in protein. Dandelion roots make a gentle but powerful hepatic system (liver and digestion) cleanser. These important body organs help remove the funky stuff that we put into our body through our food, water, and air. I think most folks will agree that, these days, there's plenty of funky stuff in there.

OBSERVATION

Even the most militant junk-food eaters love the taste of purslane and, usually, lamb's quarter. The interesting thing about the taste of wild plants is that once people begin to try them, they begin to crave them. No surprise there: your body knows what it needs. It's your mind that gets in the way, and perhaps one too many excellent marketing strategies. I mean, really, only excellent marketing could get a person to try Pop Rocks!

CONSIDER

Beginning to incorporate wild foods into your daily diet is the very best way that you can get good, natural, local food. Wild food is not brought to you from far distances, requiring huge amounts of energy to transport; it's not picked before it's fully nutritious in order to be able to be shipped to you unbruised; and it's not packaged up in all sorts of interesting materials that create a waste problem. It is, however, of superior nutritional quality compared to most food found in stores, even the most organic, natural, non-GMO-grown food you can buy.

When we take just a moment to consider the water and air quality in the areas where most of our agricultural land is situated—no matter how natural or organic it is advertised to be—it isn't hard to be persuaded to go out and harvest your own dinner. You'll also get a whole lot more exercise going out and hunting down and harvesting the plants you want to eat than you ever will pushing a wheeled cart down the aisles of a grocery store.

That's another thing this beautiful body of ours was designed to do—move. When we become modern grazers, we eat, move, and experience the outdoors in just the way that this incredible body, this marvel of engineering, was made to do. No wonder it feels so good!

PREPARING WILD FOODS

Now that we've looked at free food, let's look at how to use it. Besides eating it raw, we can preserve it for later.

DRYING TO PRESERVE

Drying the wild foods you find allows you to incorporate good nutrition into your meals year-round. I hang bundles of nettle, lamb's quarter, and amaranth in my root cellar during the summer. I cut bunches before they seed; the leaves are most nutritious before the plant gives its energy to producing the seed. Then I can grab a handful of dried leaves whenever I need them, crumbling them up into my stews, sauces, soups, chilis, salsas, omelets, or whatever else I'm cooking. I also harvest seed from these plants when the seeds darken and add that seed to lots of things including bread.

PICKLING PURSLANE

Purslane is so good raw and chopped up into anything, and one of my favorite ways to use it is in potato salad. To enjoy purslane throughout the year, pickling it is wonderful! I chop it up, add whole garlic, bits of carrot or whatever, cover it in pickling brine, and process it in a glass jar using a water-bath canning method. In most grocery stores, you can find the *Ball Blue Book Guide to Preserving* near where they sell canning jars. If you don't know how to can yet, learn. It is too much fun—science, creativity, and yumminess all together. What a great way to spend some time and create unique recipes.

RAW AND STEAMED GREENS

After picking nettle leaves (with gloves on), I steam them before eating. Dandelion leaf is eaten raw when young and new. If you don't mind a slightly bitter taste, you can even eat it once it ages, before the flowering. As the leaves mature and darken, they are better when steamed and tossed with yummy oils or sauces and mixed with grated cheese or other vegetables. It is so good for our bodies that it is one of those tastes you should cultivate!

➤

DANDELION ROOT TEA

I dig the roots before the flower head forms, so the good medicine energy is still in the root and not going into making a flower. Then I chop the roots into small chunks, put them into my old-fashioned wire-mesh popcorn popper, and roast them gently over the coals of the fire until they turn a deep golden brown. You can do this in your oven at home, keeping a close eye, at about 250°F. These roasted chunks make a hearty tea that is the most gentle and effective hepatic system cleanser I know.

HEALTH TIP

The dandelion flowers can be collected on a bright spring or summer morning to make an excellent, very mild fermented drink that acts as a gentle cleansing tonic for the liver and kidney, when needed. There are many wonderful recipes to be found for this drink, and my favorite one uses slices of orange.

DANDELION

Dandelion Tonic

1 gallon dandelion blooms
Boiled water, to cover
2 pounds cane sugar
$^1/_2$ pound honey
3 to 4 unpeeled lemons, chopped
3 to 4 unpeeled oranges, chopped
2 ($^1/_4$-ounce) packages yeast

Pick your open, perfect dandelion blooms early in the morning when the dew still clings to the flowers. Place the flowers into a 2-gallon or larger crock and pour in boiled water to cover the flowers. Cover the crock with cheesecloth and let sit at room temperature for 3 days.

Squeeze the juice from the flowers, and then transfer the flower liquid to a large pot. Compost the flower heads. Add the cane sugar, honey, lemons, and oranges to the liquid. Cover the pot and boil the liquid for 30 minutes. Allow the flower mixture to cool until lukewarm, and then pour it into a crock and stir in the yeast. Cover the crock with cheesecloth and let brew for 2–3 weeks, until the yeasty bubbling stops.

Boil 12 (1-quart) canning jars and lids for 10 minutes to sterilize. Cover the jar opening with cheesecloth and pour the flower liquid into the jars. Cap the jars with the sterilized seals and rings and let sit in a cool, dark place for 1-2 months. The amount of jars needed will depend on the final amount of dandelion tonic after fermentation, which varies. I like to drink this tonic chilled.

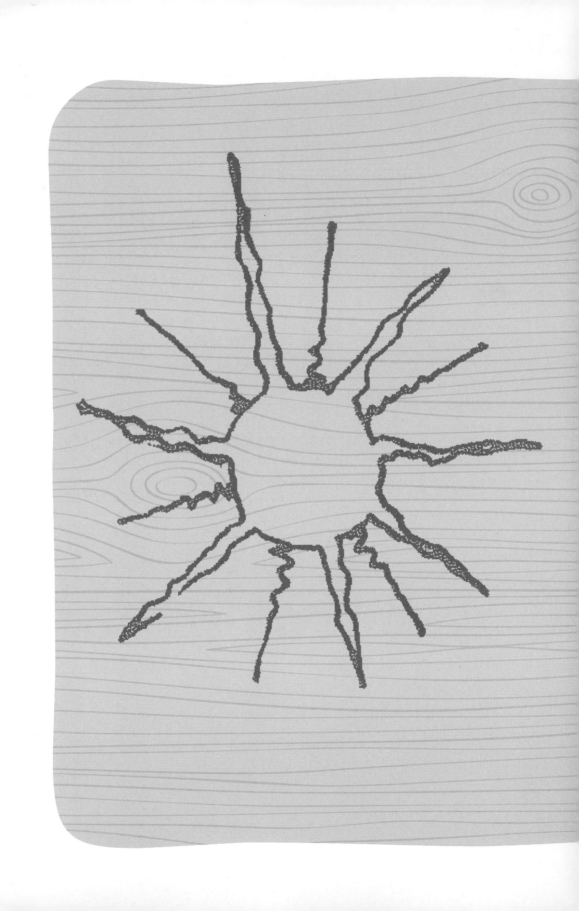

COOKING AND DEHYDRATING WITH THE SUN

No matter where you live, if it isn't a cloudy day, you have free energy from the sun to cook your meals. For decades now, modern society has been thinking on, arguing about, and rallying around the cause of environmental preservation. It is a mystery to me why every newly constructed home, whether on a solid foundation or wheels, doesn't come equipped with a solar oven, or why every household doesn't have a solar cooker on their porch, patio, sidewalk, in their backyard, or even in their camping gear. It would be a great way to walk the talk of doing something to keep the environment healthy. Give that some thought.

There are lots of solar-oven manufacturers, solar-cooking manuals, and companies selling solar-cooking products. A wonderful design called the All American Sun Oven is made by Sun Ovens International. If you want to try out this fantastic way of cooking your meals, which is really just a whole lot of fun and combines all kinds of science, engineering, and creativity, there are plenty of resources for you to research. (See Resources, p. 302.)

GOOD NEWS

If you're really not interested in having one more appliance around, or you simply don't have room in your budget to think about acquiring a manufactured solar cooker (or spending even less money on the simple materials to build your own), the sun is still right there to do lots of things for you. It can make fruit and vegetable leathers, seed and nut bars, or tea infusions. Many folks already use the simple steps of placing their loose leaf tea or tea bags into a clear glass jar and setting it into the sun for several hours.

You can also simply wrap leftovers or precooked food in foil, or place it in a little dark pot with a glass lid, and place it in just the right spot of sunshine to quickly warm up. This takes about half an hour in direct sunlight. As long as the food is rising in temperature, there is no risk in it sitting out too long.

Bonus! You get to do a lot of this outdoors. It's the perfect opportunity to be immersed in the environmental conditions that grew your beautiful body. You are getting healthier, both physically and emotionally, by the minute!

CREATE A FRUIT LEATHER

Fruit and vegetable leathers are very easy to make. Simply take your foodstuffs, blend them together, and pour the mixture out into a thin layer in a large rimmed baking pan or cookie sheet. You can mix and match any kind of fruit and vegetables you want.

Take the pan outside to a place that stays sunny all day long. Depending on where you live and how strong the sun is that day, the top surface will dry up and shrink slightly away from the edges. This might take several days in a row or only a few hours. Just keep checking on it.

When the top of the leather is dry, flip it over and let the opposite side dry. If you need it to dry more quickly, take a pizza slicer and cut the fruit or vegetable mat into strips, just like the kind you buy in the store.

You can also dry your leather in a sunny window, in a manufactured or homemade food dehydrator, or on a very low heat setting in your electric or gas oven.

Fruit and vegetable leathers are healthy and convenient when you don't feel like cooking. They are easy to make, store, carry, and eat. You can up their nutritional value by adding some of the dried leaves of those five wonderful plants. (See Gather Wild Food in the City, p. 57.)

QUESTION

Remember what they are? **Lamb's quarter**, **purslane**, **amaranth**, **nettle**, and **dandelion**. Use the dried leaf when making the leathers, as the fresh leaf, being a wild plant, is resilient and won't dry out as easily in the mixture.

IMPORTANT

If you don't intend to refrigerate them or you can't eat them all at once, make sure the fruit leathers are well cured. They will last much longer if they are thoroughly dried out.

TIP

If you're setting these leathers outside to dry, cover the tray or pan with a double layer of cheesecloth. A small package of cheesecloth can be found in almost every store that sells kitchen gadgets. Using a cheesecloth cover keeps flies, as well as dust and debris that might be in the air, off the food but still allows the moisture to evaporate quickly.

SEED AND NUT BARS

Dried seed and nut bars can be made in a very similar way. Take your collected seeds and nuts, grind them down into smaller pieces as needed, add them to some kind of sticky mixture that will help hold them all together—like a bowl of soaked flax seeds that has become very gelatinous or okra that's been smashed and cooked down—or simply add them to any of the fruit and vegetable leathers you are making. It's that simple.

REMEMBER

Every time you make a choice to incorporate even the smallest amount of wild plants, which grow in almost all environments, into your modern diet, you are taking a simple, doable, affordable step towards greatly improved health and well-being.

TRICKS AND TIPS FOR TELLING A GOOD STORY

Long before video streaming, television, movie theaters, radio, printed books, handwritten books, scrolls and parchments, hieroglyphics, and cave paintings, we were enthralling and educating each other by telling stories. We were telling stories even before we had thoughtfully structured and complicated language systems.

OPINION

I think it's fair to say that oral storytelling is on the list of endangered arts (unless you're a political speechwriter). However, visual media is the storytelling of our time. Through the many media outlets technology offers us, stories large and small, grand or humble, pertinent or frivolous, are told.

CONSIDER

Having a story delivered through technological means is a very different experience from the interactions our ancestors shared when telling and listening to stories in the night hours around the campfire, huddled under animal hides on a long winter night, while gathering or preparing plants and berries for a meal, or while covering the many miles of a migration route leading to summer hunting. This kind of personal, interactive storytelling is what we have an opportunity to share and experience while playing in the woods. Without access to electronics or movies or even printed books, we have an opportunity to engage in the art of storytelling.

OBSERVATION

Modern culture fosters specialization, and this is seen in modern storytelling. A cadre of celebrities—actors and performers, showcased songwriters, singers, and musicians whose work monopolizes the airwaves, TV hosts, comedians, and recognized public speakers—are who most of us consider worthy of being allowed to tell our stories. The very best stories I have ever heard have been shared by the most unpolished performers and blurted out in the most unlikely circumstances.

OPINION
What a gift we can give each other, telling and listening to each other's stories. Jokes, songs, fantasies, and accounting of actual events bring joy and camaraderie to families, friends, and communities. If we let go of the idea of having to be good at it and just start sharing and listening, we can experience the richness and joy of oral storytelling.

CONSIDER
A beautiful song called *Tell Me Again*, written by Scott Martin has a chorus I think of often:

> *Won't you tell me again how it goes,*
> *This story that only you know,*
> *Forgive me what I claim to know,*
> *And when it ends,*
> *Tell me again.*

It reminds me that the art of storytelling requires good listeners as well as good tellers. Everyone, young and old, has something to share that is worth learning about. Good listeners can give the gift of honoring the teller and helping them remember that they are worthy and beautiful, even if they are not a celebrity.

HISTORY
People on this planet have been telling their stories over and over again since time began. Repetition keeps memory strong, maintains accurate knowledge, solidifies community, strengthens the sense of belonging to something bigger than ourselves, and brings delight in the expectation of a sagacious punch line, a moral conclusion, or an ironic twist.

QUESTION
Have you noticed how a child asks for the same story over and over again? Certainly, this desire for repetition is developmental, but I believe it is also genetic.

HISTORY
For millennia, we have shared stories that teach us how to do the things we need to do to stay alive, how to discern the character of people who might be trying to

trick us, and to believe in the interconnectedness of all living things, the strength of which comes to our aid in times of need. These stories teach us to learn from mishaps (and laugh about them later) and to treat our loved ones with honor, loyalty, and respect, which ultimately brings us deep joy and satisfaction in life. Through stories we learn to face our fears with determination and bravery, find creative solutions, be grateful, and work together.

Oral storytelling was our ancestors' version of a 101 college class. Repeat, repeat, repeat. The information was never outdated, even though the faces and names changed, and passing it along was important for survival. It was also a record of our history and an honoring of those who came before us, those who made wise decisions that allowed us all to continue. Without the written word, it was repetition that allowed our stories to survive long after individuals had passed. So go ahead, read that kids' book for the seventh time in a row. You'll be carrying on an honorable, ancient tradition!

TELL A GOOD STORY

Storytelling is a more fun when it captures and keeps our attention, even if we are hearing a serious tale or being educated. Practice some of these techniques on your friends and family.

VOICE TRICKS

Tell your story in a voice other than your own. Depending on the story or character, make your voice high, low, gruff, or syrupy sweet. This alone will increase interest.

SOUND EFFECTS

If you say, "We started walking through the mud," pause before you continue, and then make messy, sucky noises like tennis shoes squelching into the muck. Perhaps you are telling how the whole family fell asleep. Make loud, humorous, repetitious snoring sounds, and then look at your audience with an "it's our little secret" glance and say conspiratorially, "Grandma was snoring!"

SPOOKY NOISES

If you are telling a story about a frightening experience, perhaps sneaking into an abandoned house, make soft, eerie creaking noises after you say you moved past the rotten door hanging off one hinge.

ANIMAL SOUNDS

Maybe you are telling a story about the time you went deer hunting, and it turns out you were in competition with a mountain lion that's waiting in the tree next to you for the same deer you see approaching. Before you tell the part where you look up to see the mountain lion, make the soft purring noises that alerted you to the animal.

INSTRUMENT USE (RATTLES, DRUMS, AND WHISTLES)

Let's say your story is about a rattlesnake, a frog, and a squirrel.

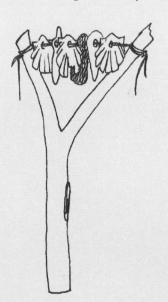

Tell the story using instruments for the animals without ever using their names. "Once there was a (shake the rattle) sneaking up on a (beat the drum softly several times) to eat him for dinner. Every time the (shake the rattle) got close to the (beat the drum), a little (blow the whistle shrilly with a trilling sound) would sound the alarm." This really makes folks listen closely, and they have fun guessing what the animals are.

MOVEMENT AND SURPRISE MOTIONS

If you use repetitive hand motions for certain sounds or activities that are repeated throughout the story, the audience begins to unconsciously join in, and everyone has more fun. Clap your hands loudly if you mention thunder, or leap forward and roll if you are talking about jumping off a train. Surprises bring your audience to immediate attention and make your delivery entertaining.

Next time you head out into the woods, try out some of these storytelling tricks and leave the technology behind, even if you do have signal!

MEMORY

When I was a kid, grown-ups said, "Go play outside." So that is where we went, to play free and wild, to imagine and make up stories, and to act out those stories in great drama games below the lilac bushes, which were castles or log cabins or labyrinths under the Roman Colosseum, perhaps. We played in and around weedy, abandoned city lots that became the rolling prairie plains that we crossed in a covered wagon (with a broken wheel) full of baby pigs and crying children, and—wait! Was that thundering sound imminent death by lightning or a herd of angry buffalo? Then you come running home for dinner, excited and sweaty and full of wonder. You're trying to tell the story, but you only hear "Use your inside voice." "Go wash your hands." "Settle down and do your schoolwork."

RESULT

And so our storytelling panache is eroded away.

MENTOR

Marilyn Kinsella is a professional storyteller with many wonderful stories. She has a wonderful trick for making the sound of a baby crying. She wads up a piece of cloth, and then, turning her head away from her listeners, she wails into the cloth, doing three long whaaa, whaaa, whaaa noises and a hitched up, hiccup kind of breath. It sounds so real! In another story that captivates us all, she talks about one particular character, and she rolls her eyes around and around in great big circles, just like the character is doing in the story. These effects keep us riveted to the plot.

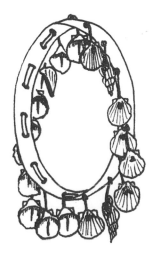

MORE STORYTELLING TIPS

STEREO SOUND EFFECTS

You can plan ahead to tell the story and get friends to help you play out the parts. Have your friends sit around in different places with all the other listeners. At certain points in the story, have them make the sound effects. It's like primitive stereo, and there's this feeling that the story is encompassing the group. Perhaps they all shout out together if you're talking about an angry crowd coming down the road, and then they let their voices soften and fade away as the crowd is leaving the storyline.

DISTANCE SOUND EFFECTS

Perhaps someone closest to the back of the crowd is a very loud train whistle when your story talks about the train coming through. Then another friend blows the whistle a little bit more softly, somewhere in the middle of the listeners, and finally the whistle is blown very quietly up at the front of the audience. You can do this with a dog barking in the distance and coming closer as well, or the sound of a large animal walking away into the night. Effects like this make you feel like you're really in the story.

INSTRUMENT EFFECTS

You can collect a basket of things that make great sound effects. A small metal washboard gives you wonderful options. A harmonica, a wooden train whistle, bells, a small xylophone, flutes, and rattles of varying sizes are all great sound effects tools to put in the basket.

CALL AND RESPONSE TECHNIQUE

Another really fun thing to do is to involve your listeners through call and response storytelling. Let's say your story is about a child named Jimmy Boy, whose mother is always calling him back in just as he's getting out the garden gate. Before you begin the story, you can tell the group that throughout the story the mother will be calling, "Ohhhh, Jimmy Boy!" Of course you will be using your best high-pitched, silly mommy voice. Tell the group that each time they hear you call this out, they need to respond in unison, "Coming, Mother!" Of course, you can apply this idea to any story you want to, and it makes it all so much more fun.

WILD MEDICINAL PLANTS AND TEA INFUSIONS

MAKE WILD HERB TEA

GATHER THE HERBS, JAR, AND LID
First you need the plants that you want to infuse. In Gather Wild Food in the City, p. 57, we talked about where and when to gather wild plants, and how to begin learning to identify the plants in your area. My very favorite tea mix is nettle leaves, red clover leaves and blossoms, and raspberry leaves. It tastes great iced or warm. Then you need a 1-quart canning jar with the seal and ring cap, or any top that fits well. If you have dried these plants ahead of time, you'll need a "goodly" handful of each.

QUESTION

What does that mean? For me, a goodly handful is filling the center of your cupped palm with a little pile of dried herb. I collect, preserve, and cook wild plants, so I am always being asked, "How much of this do you put in?" and "What amount of such and such?" or "Is that a 1/2 cup?" I really have no idea. I just go for it! Besides, wild plants don't come in set measurements, forms, conditions, or sizes.

KNOWLEDGE

Wild plants don't even contain the same amounts of nutrition from plant to plant or season to season. So much depends on the nutrition of the soil they grow in, which varies from place to place and year to year, and the water and light they receive. If you think about it, people are the same way.

FILL THE JAR
If you've dried the plant ahead of time, add that goodly handful of mixed herbs to the jar. If you are picking them fresh, fill your jar about halfway with equal portions of each leaf.

BOIL THE WATER
Now, set that jar close by, with the cap at hand, and boil some water. When the water is boiling, pour it over the leaves waiting in the jar. Immediately cap the jar once you have poured the boiling water over it.

Did you get that? **Do not** boil the leaves in the water! Boil the water separately, and then pour it over the leaves in the canning jar.

KNOWLEDGE

By immediately capping the jar, you trap the rising steam and prevent it from escaping the jar with many of the good things that are in the plant. Often, when people make a cup of tea, many of the good properties of the tea mix are lost to the air if they don't cover the cup while the tea bag steeps. It's still good tea, but it's not nearly as much of a superfood as it could be.

IMPORTANT

When you make a tea infusion like this, use an official canning jar. These are easy to find at your local grocery store. Canning jar manufacturers have put much thought and science into the creation of a glass jar that can withstand quick temperature changes without cracking. Recycling an empty mayonnaise or salsa jar is tempting, but save those for storing dried plant leaves, seeds, or berries. They are not designed or manufactured like a canning jar. You might get away with using them a few times, but you might not. You really don't need that much excitement in the kitchen.

INFUSING THE HERBS

Once you have filled and capped the jar, let it set in a cool place for 6–8 hours. Pour the liquid through a strainer over ice and enjoy like iced tea. You can also drink it warm. Pour the liquid into a pot or kettle, and heat it carefully. So the nutrition won't be compromised, cover the warming pot with a lid, and make sure the liquid does not boil.

NOTE

Use a strainer! If you're trying raspberry leaves in your tea mix, make sure to use a fine strainer. The raspberry leaf has fine little hairs that catch in your throat if you don't strain the tea. It will feel like you're trying to swallow chalk! Rose hips, the lovely little red fruit that comes on in the fall after the rose blossom has faded, can have the same effect if the outer fleshy covering breaks open to expose the fuzzy seeds inside, so strain them well. Other than rose hips and raspberry leaves, I haven't used any other tea plants that have the same issue. Anyway, you'll learn all this yourself as you sample, create, and enjoy learning about the plants that are here, aiding and encouraging you to become the healthiest body you can be.

TUMMY ACHE REMEDY

MAKE YOUR OWN MEDICINE

Make a simple 1-quart jar infusion of mint leaves next time you have a little tummy ache. Peppermint works well, but horsemint and spearmint are also effective tummy calmers. You don't have to let this one sit for 6–8 hours before using it, but you can. It's just that when you want a tummy calmer, you usu-ally want it right away. Fortunately, most of the mints are strong enough to be helpful, even after a short period of steeping.

STORAGE

Put whatever you don't use in a cool, dark space for use within 24 hours, or store it in the refrig-erator. Most infusions will last up to a week in a cold place, or a bit longer if you first strain the plant material from the liquid. If you strain the plant material after the first 6–8 hours of steeping,

MINT

you can often pour boiling water over the plant material again, and even though it will have less of the medicinal and nutritional qualities you're hoping for, it will still taste good and offer some nutritional benefits.

CONSIDER

Whenever I'm done making my plant infusions, I dump the plant materials directly into a pot of soup or stew. If nothing like this is bubbling on the fire or stove, I put the leaves into my garden beds or around my fruiting or flowering bushes and trees. If you have a plant-infusion liquid that is no longer fresh and doesn't taste good, don't pour it down the drain; rather, empty the contents into your house-plants, garden, or yard. If you don't have any of those, pour it in the grass or weeds around where you live. You'll probably want a lot of those weeds to grow anyway, now that you know how great they are. Perhaps you keep chickens; pour the tired infusion into their water pan.

KIDS TUMMY REMEDY

MAKE A CALMING TEA FOR CHILDREN

Catnip makes a gentle tummy tea for children. Catnip is also a general calming tonic for children. This is interesting when we consider what it does to cats! However, children aren't cats—although many of them like to behave like cats (or puppies, roosters, or monkeys)—so catnip, instead of exciting their nervous system, actually calms them down. This is a comfort for weary parents and other adults who care for children.

Other plants you can use for calming tea infusions are motherwort, chamomile, and linden flower (basswood).

BASSWOOD

HOW TO MAKE A DRUM

Have you been jammin' on your sticks and stones? Perhaps you've used your sticks like a pair of drumsticks and noticed the difference when you tap them along on a solid object compared to when you tapped them on something hollow. You tap them on something hollow that is cracked, and you get a completely different sound than when you tap them on something that has solid sides and top.

IDEA

This full, dense, reverberating sound you hear when you tap the solid-sided hollow space pulls at the heart, mesmerizes the mind, and has been enticing us to be creative drum makers for a very long time. Our body is constantly moving to a steady rhythm: the heartbeat inside. It is the first thing a growing baby feels and hears. It's no surprise that most people are drawn to the sound of the drum.

Music universally calls us, pulls us in, and sweeps us into a large spectrum of emotions; a baseline beat is a part of who we all are. Drums have also been used in complicated communication systems, like the talking drums of Africa, during periods of civil resistance. I guess we could even call Morse code a kind of drumming. Making drums is a lot of fun, and playing them is even more fun.

ROLE MODEL

Musical adults generally bring up musical children. Young ones immersed in just about anything seem to pick up the skills and abilities that surround them with no apparent effort. What we do is so much more important than what we say. Go figure!

Children love to imitate. If you'll start drumming or get excited about making some drums, your children will have a lot of fun with it too, and perhaps they'll even develop a skill that enriches their lives. By demonstrating healthy, happy activities and lifestyles, you are communicating the strongest message you can send. Besides, *you* are also having fun and developing skills and abilities that allow *you* to feel capable and confident. Good deal!

START DRUMMING

Start at home by setting some pots and pans and Tupperware upside down on the kitchen floor, and then pass out the wooden spoons. This is actually a good way to have fun and learn to drum, even when there are not any children around. Taking this idea out to the backyard, you can tip over some 5-gallon plastic buckets or your rubber or metal trashcans and get a great drum session started.

INSPIRATION

Making incredible music and touring the country, Billy Jonas jams with a collection of instruments he makes from things at home or from the recycle pile. He plays many at once! His creative arrangements, unique rhythms, and wonderful lyrics make his music irresistible. He's made a lot of great CDs that kids, teens, and adults love. You don't need to be a celebrity to be an awesome musician. (See Resources, p. 302.)

SIMPLE DRUMMING

Take some time to head into the woods and start looking for instrument opportunities. Hollow logs are easy to find and make a great start for drums. You can play them just like and where they are, lying horizontal on the ground with both ends open. Use the percussion sticks you made in Make Music with Sticks and Stones, p. 7, or pick up a couple of branches with some weight for your drumsticks. Heavier branches will give a deeper sound.

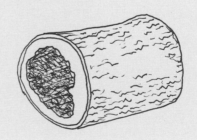

CONSIDER

Drumming can actually be a part of increasing your comfort in the outdoors.

HERE'S HOW

In the area you choose to go most often, perhaps a place where you've created your own secret spot or the place you go for wild food foraging, you can set up a collection of hollow log drums.

Perhaps one day you get turned around in that area and don't have a good idea of how to get back to where you started. You could start playing one of those drums, and it would work like a signaling device. If anyone is looking for you, they could come to the sound of the drum. If someone who isn't looking for you goes by, they might be drawn in by the rhythm you are playing.

IDEA TO TRY

You could work out this whole system with your friends or your family, and you could communicate through the drums in different places around the area. Let's say you're late coming home, and a friend or family member starts to worry about you. Perhaps you've just lost track of time because you're so engrossed in the mushrooms you just found, or you've just found some rocks that will make perfect stone knives. Your friend could come into the area they know you usually wander in, and if you have set up a hollow-log drum near an entry to the area (where everyone knows where it is) they could begin beating out a rhythm on that hollow log. When you hear it, you could go right away to the closest place you have another hollow log drum and beat back in response. That would calm everybody down.

If you actually are turned around, and you heard the drum beating, you could follow the sound of the drum, letting the sound lead you to your friend. You could also set up this drum system just for fun, each player having a particular rhythm that identifies them.

MAKING A DRUM

MAKE A DRUM TOP

You can get a bigger sound from that same hollow log. If it's short enough to tip upright so that you can still reach the top once you steady the bottom in the ground, you can place a thick bark slab over the open top. If the slab doesn't bounce around too much, you can beat on it and get that deep, hollow drum sound. You can carve the slab, using your stone knife, into a circular shape that sits inside the lip of the log without falling down inside. Tap it into place a little bit to set it in.

RAWHIDE DRUM TOP

Most drums we see have a top cover of some kind of animal hide. Skin coverings give your drum a wonderful full sound. Rawhide is what is most often used to make a drumhead. For a big hollow-log drum, you need a big piece of rawhide. However, you can make drums of all sizes, and it is very easy to purchase rawhide from any leather provider, like Moscow Hide and Fur or Tandy Leather.

MAKE A DRUM BASE

You can make a drum base from lots of different materials. If you live in an area of the Southwest where big agave plants grow, you can cut off the base of the dead stalks to the desired height you want and put a covering over one or both ends of the base. To make a drum base out in the woods, take 6 or 8 flat pieces of wood and bind them together in a hexagon or octagon shape. If you don't have wood or an agave plant on hand, you can build your own drum base with clay.

USE YOUR STONE OR STEEL KNIFE

You can split slats of wood off a bigger log or branch with your stone or steel knife. Once you have the number of wooden slats you want, make sure they are all the same length. Use your knife blade to flatten the short edges of the slats (the top and bottom edges that will sit on the ground and get covered with a drumhead) and remove any sharp points. Then use your knife blade to bevel the two long edges of each slat.

BEVEL THE EDGE

When you bevel an edge, you are carving it at an angle from its original flat cut. We are beveling (or angling) the edge of our slats so that when we put them together, with the vertical edges pressing flat against each other without gaps, they form a (six-sided) hexagon or an (eight-sided) octagon. If you view each slat from the top or bottom edge, it should look like a horizontally long, vertically skinny trapezoid. (If you're homeschooling right now, rest assured that you are getting your fourth-grade geometry curriculum as you do this project.)

When you split your flat wooden slats off a larger log or branch, the vertical edges may already be somewhat beveled. However, you are just randomly splitting them off with your knife, so there's no real way to know exactly what the edges will look like. At any rate, you know you want to bevel the edges so that they join together tightly with as few gaps as possible; this will give you a better sound.

FIND SOME STRING-MAKING PLANTS

Once you have your slats made, scout about for some good string-making plants (see Make String and Rope from Plant Fibers, p. 15). Make a strong length of plant string that will wrap around your drum base two or three times. Place the slats together in their final shape, using the dirt on the ground to help prop them, and secure your plant string around the outside. You'll be at this for a little while, but how many people do you know who can say they walked out into the woods and made their own drum base?

KNOWLEDGE
PITCH GLUE

Once you know how to make a fire and be very safe with it out in the woods (see Light a One-Match Campfire, p. 151), you'll have the ability to use the flames to melt tree pitch. Pitch is that sappy syrup that gets all over you when you climb trees or drops into your hair or clothing when you walk under branches that have recently broken or been sawed off. If you can collect a good amount of this sap or pitch and melt it on the flame, you can use it like glue—it's the original hot glue.

COLLECTING PITCH TO MAKE GLUE

When I go pitch collecting, I carry a tin can (the kind food comes in at the grocery store) and a table knife from the kitchen. You could also grab a metal paint scraper from the shop. Neither of these implements are very sharp, so they are safe for collecting pitch. Before you go, grease the blade of the table knife or scraper with shortening from the kitchen or bearing grease from the shop. Maybe take a little extra greasing material with you. Then, when you go around prying and scraping pitch off the trees into the can, you won't get in any trouble for ruining a good table knife because it will be easy to clean off when you're done.

CLEAN YOUR PITCH-GATHERING TOOLS

If you're like me and get too excited to go out and gather pitch, forgetting to grease the blade first, then rubbing cooking oil or peanut butter on the blade when you get home helps take the sticky off the knife blade as well as off your hands. If your hands are all sticky from pitch, you're not going home anytime soon, and you didn't bring along any peanut butter, you can clean your hands with dry dirt or sand. Rub your hands together like you're washing them with the dirt or sand. The pitch will peel away like rubber cement with the layer of sand or dirt. It won't come off all at once; you will have to dip your hands back in the dirt or sand several times before you stop sticking to things.

MELTING PITCH

This would be another way you could connect the slats of your drum base. You can place a flat rock by a small fire and put the sap you collect on the rock. The sap will melt. Swirl the end of a stick into the melted pitch, and use it to smear the pitch glue up and down the vertical sides of your slats. Arrange the slats together and prop them in the way already described. You'll still want to make the plant string to hold the slats together on the outside.

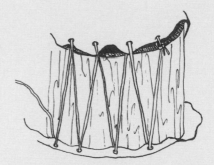

ATTACH A HIDE DRUM TOP

There are several easy ways you can attach a hide over the top of your drum. A softened piece of leather stretched very tightly over the top of a drum will make a decent sound. Even though soft leather or any kind of tight, tough fabric will work, rawhide makes the best drumheads.

CUT OUT THE RAWHIDE

Before you cut out the drumhead top from the rawhide, you need to wet it and stretch it. Cut the circular head large enough that it overlaps the drum-base edges by at least 1 or 2 inches.

KNOWLEDGE

As rawhide dries, it shrinks. The rawhide tightens and hardens on the drum base, giving it a bigger sound than soft leather or other materials.

▲▲▲
MAKING A RAWHIDE LEATHER DRUMHEAD

TACKING THE DRUM TOP IN PLACE

When you have your damp rawhide drumhead cut out and ready to put on the base, you can simply stretch it down over the base edges and tack it in place. If you're doing this out in the woods, you can poke small holes, evenly spaced, all around the exterior edge of the rawhide. Make an equal amount of little holes in the outer edge of

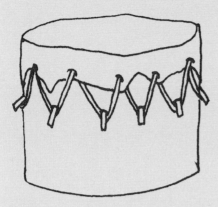

the drum base about 1 or 2 inches below the top. Cut or break small pieces of sturdy sticks or twigs and poke them through the holes in the rawhide and into the holes in the drum base. Take a little rock and hammer the sticks in place.

LACING THE DRUM TOP ON PEGS

You could also peg in a bunch of sturdy little sticks all around the drum base, about halfway down. Give them a slight angle so that the ends are pointing a little bit downward, toward the ground. Again, make equally spaced holes, all the way around the rawhide drumhead.

CUT THE LACING

Cut a nice long length of lacing from other rawhide or leather you have around. You could also use some of your handmade string, but you want to make sure it's consistently twisted and strong enough not to break as the rawhide shrinks. Run whatever string or lacing you are choosing to use into one of the holes in the drumhead and down under a peg, back up into the next hole in the rawhide, and again down and under the next peg. Continue all the way around, and after you have threaded the last hole in the rawhide, tie off the end of the lacing on the peg you started with.

DRILL AND LACE

You can also stretch the rawhide drumhead over the base and tie it in place very tightly. This works pretty well and is very quick and easy. On the last drum I made, I drilled holes through the hollow log about 3 inches down from the edge of the base; then I ran the lacing through these holes and the holes in the drumhead.

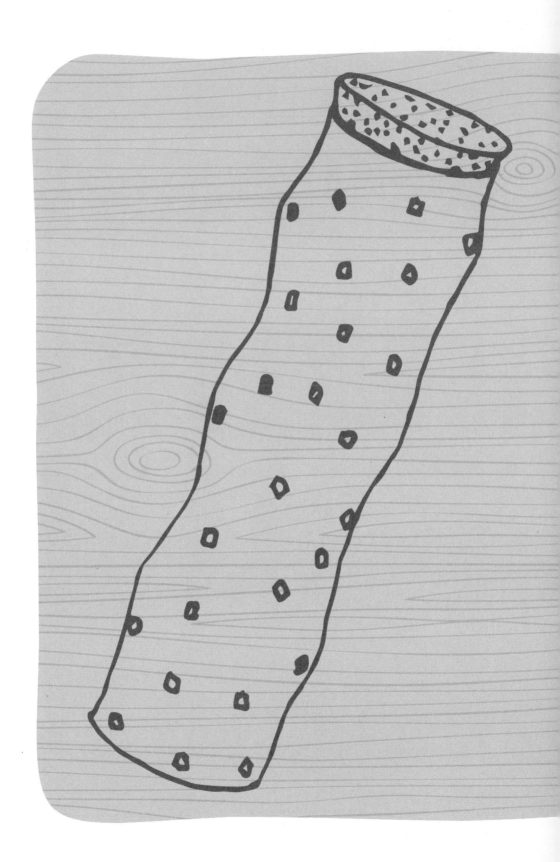

MAKE A RAINSTICK

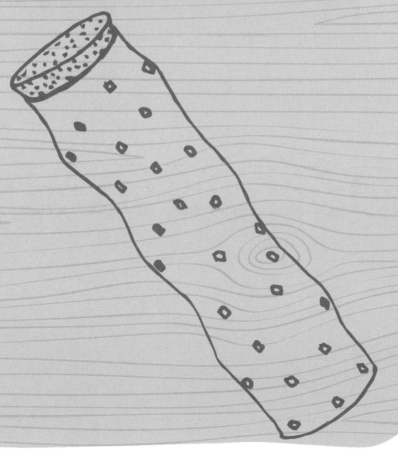

▲▲▲
MAKE A RAINSTICK

Rainsticks are another fun instrument to make in the woods. You just need some kind of a hollow tube with a little length to it and some small pebbles or seeds to put inside it. Once you put the pebbles inside the hollow tube, you seal the ends and stick little thorns or small sticks up and down the length of the tube from all sides. Then, when you tip the tube up and down, just the way you would turn an hourglass, you hear a wonderful sound, which is how it gets its name.

PLANTS TO USE
The central stalk of the agave plant is perfect for this, or you can use the bottom end of large sunflower

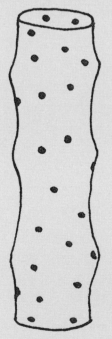
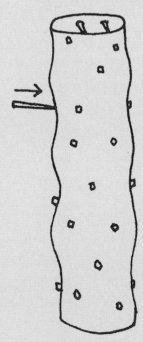

stalks. You can scrape out the pithy inside of the stalk, and then plug the ends with the same pith.

MAKE HOLES IN THE STALK
Bore little holes up and down the stalk to insert thorns or thin sticks (which allow the pebbles to bang into and bounce off of those sticks on their way down the tube, slowing them down and making a pleasant sound). Knowing how to use pitch glue (see How to Make a Drum, p. 89) can be helpful at this stage.

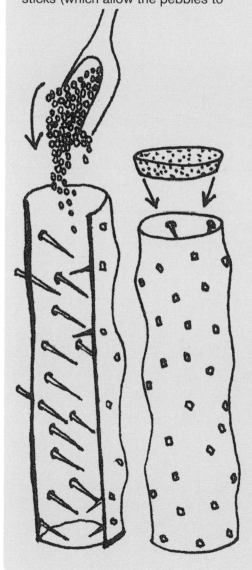

USE PITCH GLUE
A little pitch glue helps the inserted pieces stay in place. Smear pitch in the hole and then poke the little stick or thorn in all the way to the outer edge. Now smear a little more pitch at the end of the little stick or thorn.

MATERIALS AROUND THE HOUSE
If you want to make a rainstick at home, you can use paper towel or toilet paper tubes, straightened paper clips, tape, glue, and dried beans or split peas.

NOTE
A rainstick makes a wonderful addition to your storytelling presentations.

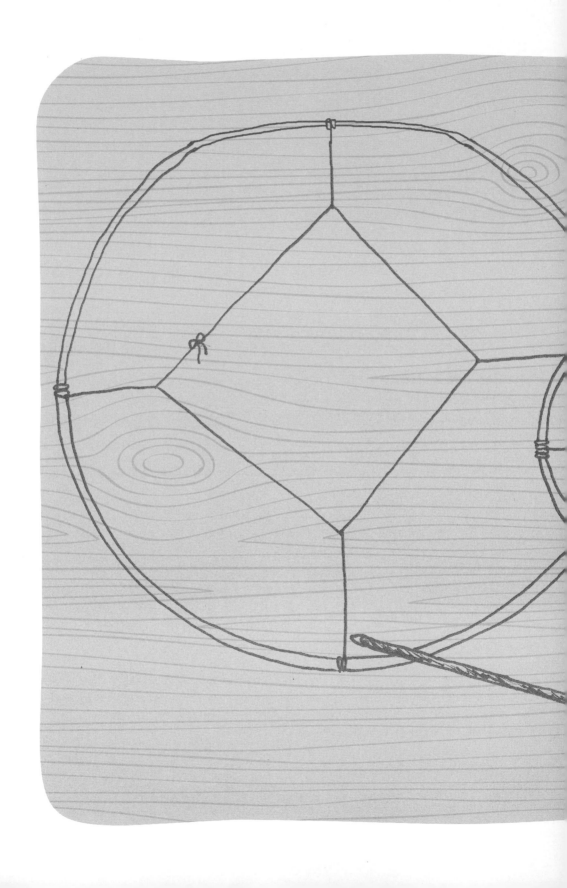

SPEAR AND HOOP GAME

We talked about throwing sticks (or rabbit sticks) and boomerangs. A spear is really just another stick you throw. Hopefully you have been practicing your aim with your throwing stick, because all that practice is going to help you when you go to chuck a spear.

HISTORY

Long before the bow and arrow (before someone thought to put a stone tip on the end of a stick), wooden spears were carved or ground to a sharp point and used to fish and hunt for animal food.

HARDENING THE TIP WITH FIRE

If you start throwing spears, you'll notice that the point begins to crumble, crack, or break very quickly. If you carve the point of your spear and then toast it over the coals, rotating it round and round as it heats up and slightly browns, you will cook the wood slightly and make it much harder, and it will last longer. You don't want to burn it, because then it turns to charcoal, gets soft, and crumbles. If you don't have a good place to make a fire, or you haven't learned to make one and maintain it safely yet, then you can just re-carve or grind your tip to sharpen it after you've thrown it a few times.

SPEAR GAME

Set up a series of targets throughout the woods and have several spears made up and ready. Run through the woods and see how many targets you can hit accurately at full speed. You can do this with a group of friends, going through the target course one at a time, and score for accuracy. After you become more accurate, you can score for time.

IMAGINE

You are the person in your clan or tribe, long, long ago, who had the responsibility to put meat on the menu. Spears and throwing sticks are the height of weapon technology in your time. You don't have any trouble taking a grouse or rabbit with a throwing stick, but today you're going after something much larger, and the throwing stick just isn't going to do the job. You are good at throwing the spear and being accurate. You've speared fish, small game, and deer.

HISTORY

When trying to interpret and understand the ancient past, logical guesses are often all we have. Archaeological evidence tells us of a possible spear-hunting technique: The hunter stood before the large prey and secured the butt end of the spear in the ground, aiming the spear point up into the animal's chest. When the animal charged to attack, and just as the animal thought it would grab you and gobble you up, it would impale itself on the spear, sending the point through its own heart. Holy smokes in a bucket! That must have taken a lot of bravery!

Perhaps holding steady as you angled your spear for the impalement of an aggravated and hungry animal towering over you took much more courage than skill, but skill was certainly required to throw your spear and kill small game and deer, requiring much practice.

QUESTION

Can you imagine? It makes me so very grateful for the grocery store!

THE HOOP GAME

Another clue in the archaeological record is the remnants of what seems to be a hoop game, possibly played between hunting forays for fun and hunting-skills development.

INSPIRATION

Evidence of this game is found on all continents. This fascinates me; not the game, though that is cool enough, but the fact that we have found evidence of a similar kind of artifact, activity, or technology on all continents. There are many pandemic (from the Greek *pandēmos,* meaning "all people") ancestral skills and technologies. More than that, people were practicing these skills and trying out these ideas at approximately the same time in the historical record.

QUESTION

Does this evidence suggest a much broader communication system than we give our caveman relatives credit for? Does it validate a theory of collective consciousness? It reminds me that we all share a heritage in these skills. I choose to concentrate on pandemic skills, instead of culturally specific skills, because they are the ones all our ancestors practiced. This history is ours—all of ours.

WILLOW HOOP GAME

COLLECT THE WILLOWS

Go out along the creeks, riverbanks, or any road ditches or irrigation canals that carry enough water throughout the year to grow willows. Take your stone knife with you and find a long, supple willow shoot that is a bit wider than your thumb at the base and doesn't have a lot of branches coming off the top. Before you cut it, bend it down into a circular shape to make sure it is flexible and doesn't crack as it bends. Cut it right near the ground. (Willows thrive when pruned, sending up several shoots from the place where they are cut back.) Trim off any smaller branching shoots up the sides or near the top.

MAKE THE HOOP

Make some string from those plants that have strong string and rope fiber (see Make String and Rope from Plant Fibers, p. 15). That string-making skill is sure coming in handy as we go, eh? Use the edge of your stone knife to make a little groove about 1 inch from the base (the thicker end) of the shoot. Then make another groove about 2 inches from the first one. Bend your willow shoot into a large hoop, like a Hula-Hoop. Make sure the shoot is long enough that the thin end is about 1 foot or more past the base when you hold it together in a circle. Tie your plant string tightly at the two grooves, which helps the plant string not slip, and you'll have a big round hoop.

PLAY THE GAME

Roll the hoop along the ground in front of you and chase after it, throwing your spear through it as it moves. The idea is that the rolling willow hoop mimics an animal that is running away from you. When you get good at this, you can modify the hoop to make the game more challenging.

MODIFY THE GAME

Make more string or use rawhide or leather strips and tie one piece from the top to the bottom of your hoop, right down the center. Then tie another piece, crossing the first piece at right angles and right in the center. You will have a big cross in the middle of your hoop, giving you four separate areas like big slices of pizza. Take a small piece of your string and tie it to secure the crossing of the two strings right in the center of the hoop. Paint the edges of the willow hoop with a different color for each pizza slice. You could also take four different strips of colored cloth or yarn and tie them around the willow edge of each area. Then you can challenge yourself to spear through only the colored area that you call out before you start.

CHALLENGE YOURSELF

Once you get good at that, you can take it even farther.

KNOWLEDGE

If you are really going hunting and hit a running animal in the leg, you might be able to go home with meat, but you might not. However, if you hit that animal in the area I call the **boilerplate**, the heart or lung area, you're much more likely to go home with food for the tribe.

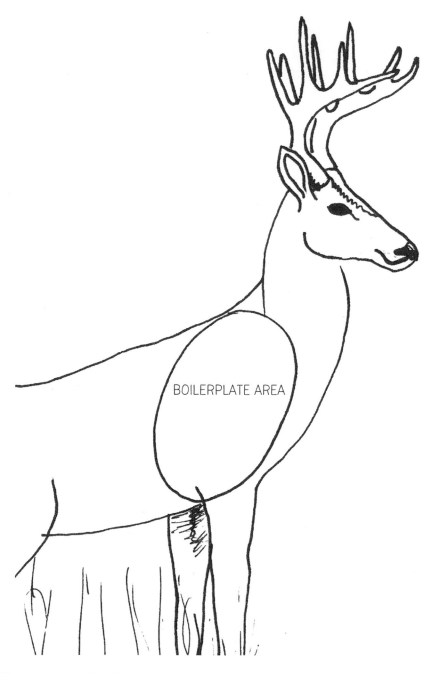

BOILERPLATE AREA

MAKE SMALLER TARGET AREAS IN YOUR WILLOW HOOP

Take two more pieces of plant string or leather strips, and tie them onto the hoop so that you have eight equal slices of pizza instead of four. (Hey homeschool folk, there's a fraction lesson!) Remember to secure the center with a tight little knot. Next, take another piece of string and tie it to one of the pizza slice strings, about one-third of the way down from the willow hoop edge to the center.

Continue tying that string to all the other strings, creating a smaller inner circle. Create an even smaller circle of string another one-third of the way down, closer to the center. You can color these areas or mark them any way you want; then you can call out which area you intend to hit before you roll the hoop. This ups the challenge and invites friendly competition.

THE PAYOFF

When you are hunting an animal, you're going to try to hit that boilerplate area. As the hoop is rolling forward, if you can hit it in the second section of the pizza slice that is at the forward side and most central of the hoop as it rolls, then you are hitting the approximate location of the animal's heart and lung area. Good news if you like to eat meat.

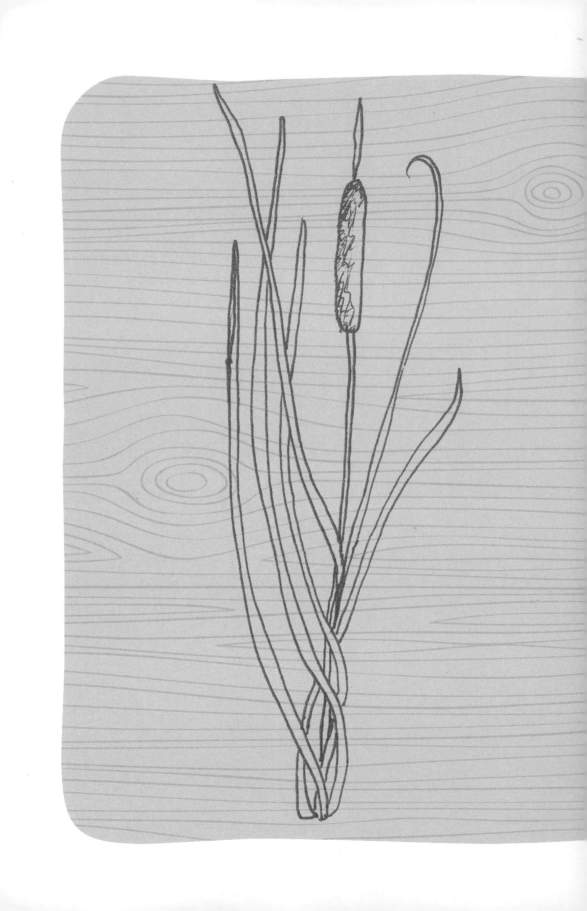

MAKE WHIP DARTS

Whip darts sound dangerous, but they are relatively safe and really fun. That's why Dick Baugh showed me how to make them when we had a group of twenty-five kids to keep busy.

The dart is made from a cattail stalk and is very lightweight. It flies really high and far, but it lands lightly, without breaking things or sticking into anything. (Take a breath, Mom!) The darts are light, simple, and well suited for children's play, but whenever I sit around and make some with folks, it is always the adults who play with them the longest.

MAKE WHIP DARTS

GATHER THE MATERIALS
You will need a cattail stalk (the central stick of the plant that holds the brown thing on top that looks like a hot dog) and one cattail leaf.

KNOWLEDGE

That hot dog thing is called the head. It makes all the seeds for the plant and, before fully maturing and tuning all fuzzy brown, is loaded with cattail pollen. This is a wonderful food source. Simply place a paper bag over the bent-down head and shake the stalk gently, letting the pollen-laden head bang around in the paper bag. Pollen will fall into the bag without removing the head from the stalk; that way you leave resources for the wild neighbors. Add the collected pollen to any flour mixture for pancakes, muffins, bread, gravy, or whatever you like.

STRING

You also need a little bit of string (see Make String and Rope from Plant Fibers, p. 15). You're good at making string by now! Make about 2½ feet. If you can find some plants that allow you to strip off a nice long piece of fiber that doesn't break, you can use that fiber without making it into string to tie on the little nub we use as a launcher for the dart.

COLLECT

With your stalk, leaf, string or fiber, and a little pitch glue (see How to Make a Drum, p. 89); you'll be ready to start.

CUT THE STALK

Cut a length of the cattail stalk a little less than 2 feet long. You can do this with your stone knife, gently cutting in all around the stalk at an angle, rotating the stalk as you make the cuts, round and round until you come to the center and have cut all the way through.

You want to be patient when cutting the length of stalk. If you cause a small break that splits up the length of the stalk, it weakens the stalk and the dart doesn't fly well.

SPLIT THE STALK END

Take your stone knife and make a 2 inch split in the thinner end of the stalk. You want both sides of the split stalk to be equal, so set the fine edge of your stone knife right on the end of the stalk in the center, and gently press it down to split the stalk open—remember, just a 2 inch split. This is where you are going to put the little folded triangle of your cattail leaf.

split cattail stalk end with stone knife

PREPARE AND GLUE THE LEAF

Take a 6 inch piece of cattail leaf and fold it into a little triangle measuring two inches on each side. Where the two ends of the leaf meet, dab a little pitch glue to hold them together, and then put a little more on the outside of each leaf end where they join. Trim the ends of the leaf triangle where they rest in the bottom of the split so they don't stick out beyond the sides of the stalk.

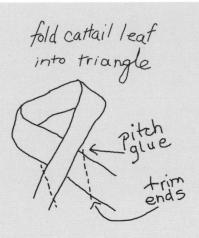

fold cattail leaf
into triangle

← pitch glue

trim ends

feathers on either side of an arrow shaft. There should be about ½ inch of the split stalk ends sticking out past the edge of the cattail leaf. This will allow you to tie a little string or fiber there to secure the split stalk after gluing it. Add a little pitch glue to the end of the insides of the split stalk ends. Ensure that the leaf is centered, and then press the split ends together.

ATTACH THE LEAF IN THE SPLIT

Carefully slide that little triangle of cattail leaf into the split on the stalk, starting with the point you just joined with pitch glue. Bring the triangle right down to the inner end of the split in the stalk. Move the triangle until it is equal on both sides of the split, looking like

TIE THE SPLIT

Use 2 (4- or 5-inch) lengths of string or fiber (enough to wrap around the cattail stalk a few times and tie a knot) to secure the glued stalk ends above the triangle leaf and at the bottom of the split where the cattail leaf sits into the split.

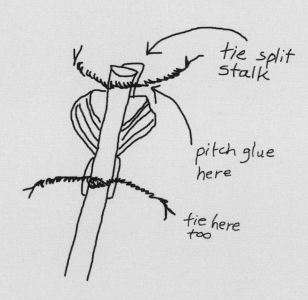

tie split stalk

pitch glue here

tie here too

KNOWLEDGE

You have just **fletched** your dart. This means you added a back rudder, of sorts, to help the dart fly better. Usually, on an arrow, feathers are used for fletching. Fletching helps an arrow or a dart fly more accurately. Thinking through how to make a thin stick of wood fly through the air more accurately, keeping the flight trajectory level and stable, is a rather high-level thought process.

CONSIDER

If you spend a moment thinking about how long ago our ancestors figured this out, it will help to dispel the stereotype of the brainless caveman.

♠♠♠
MAKE THE DART-LAUNCHING ATTACHMENT

Now you want to make a little nub that you place on your dart, about two-thirds down the length of the stalk from the front tip. This little nub will help the whip stick to launch your dart. Take a little piece of your cattail stalk, no more than 1 inch, and split it in half. Bevel the two ends of one half. You want the two beveled ends to slope out and away from each other. (Imagine you're standing at the top of a double slide, and each slide slope goes down on either side of you.) When you put the flat side up it will look like a little boat.

NOTCH THE LAUNCH NUB

Carefully use your stone knife to make a little triangular groove across (the short way) the very center of the flat side of this little boat-shaped nub. Be gentle, it's easy to break the nub. That little groove will hold the string you're going to use to tie the nub onto the dart. You don't really have to bevel the end of the nub that goes towards the tip of the dart, because it won't be the side that you loop the string of the whip stick to; however, it will fly through the air more easily if the end flying forward isn't blunt.

cut and notch the launch nub → *nub*

dart

➡

This seems rather picky for a fun activity like whip darts, but the skills you're developing will come in handy once you start getting interested in making your own arrows. The level of care you take with every detail of your arrow will make the difference between hitting the target and missing it.

GLUE THE LAUNCH NUB

Put some pitch glue on the rounded side of the nub. Press the nub onto the dart shaft, about two thirds of the way down from the tip of the dart, so that the nub is closer to the cattail-leaf fletching than the front tip. Also, place the nub so that it is not on the dart directly under the thin edge of either side of the cattail-leaf fletching, but rather, when you look right at the nub on the dart,

the two sides of the cattail leaf are going off to the left and the right. This means that when you whip the dart, the fletching will be horizontal as the dart starts to fly. Take another piece of string, wrap it securely into the groove in the nub, and tie a small flat knot. Now your dart is ready!

MAKE THE WHIP STICK

Find any stick about 3 feet long. It doesn't matter what kind of stick it is or how it looks. It's fine if it has a little bit of flex in it, but a rigid stick works too. The thicker end of the stick is the one you will hold on to, but it doesn't matter if one side of the stick is thinner or thicker. It will still work. If you have a thinner end, make a groove about 1 inch from the top with your stone knife. You're going to tie a string here,

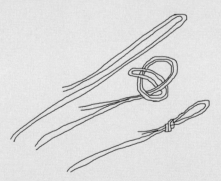

↑ tie a loop to hook the nub
  for the whip stick string

and you don't want it to slip off the end of the stick when you whip the dart.

MORE STRING

Now it's time to make more string with that fiber. You need enough string that you can tie a little loop on one end of the stick that will hook onto your little nub, wrap it around the groove in your whip stick, and tie a knot on the other end, leaving about 1 1/2 feet of string in between. Once you've wrapped one end of the string around the groove and tied a tight knot, you can form the loop for the other end of the string by simply folding over about 2 inches of the string back down onto itself and tying an overhand knot in the doubled area of the string. Make sure you have enough of a loop to hook over the little end of the nub closest to your cattail-leaf fletching.

TIME TO LAUNCH!

Hook the loop of your string over the end of the nub closest to your cattail-leaf fletching. Hold the whip stick with your dominant hand. Lightly pinch the tip of the dart between the thumb and finger of your other hand. Hold the tip up

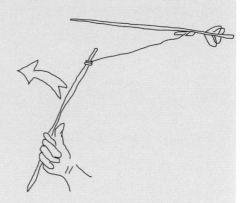

above your head, with the dart horizontal in the air and over to the side of your whip stick hand, kind of above your shoulder. (Your whip stick is held rather like you're about to swat a fly.) You should be pushing forward with a little tension on the whip stick, pulling the string tied to the end of it taut so that it's giving resistance to the dart where it's attached to the nub. You're pushing the dart backwards as you pinch the tip, while you're pulling the string taut and putting forward pressure on the whip stick. When this opposing tension is just right, whip the stick forward like you're swatting a fly, letting go of the tip of the dart at the exact same moment, and let the loop of the string fling the dart into the air.

You are going to be surprised. Keep your eye on that flying dart. It probably won't be that easy to find.

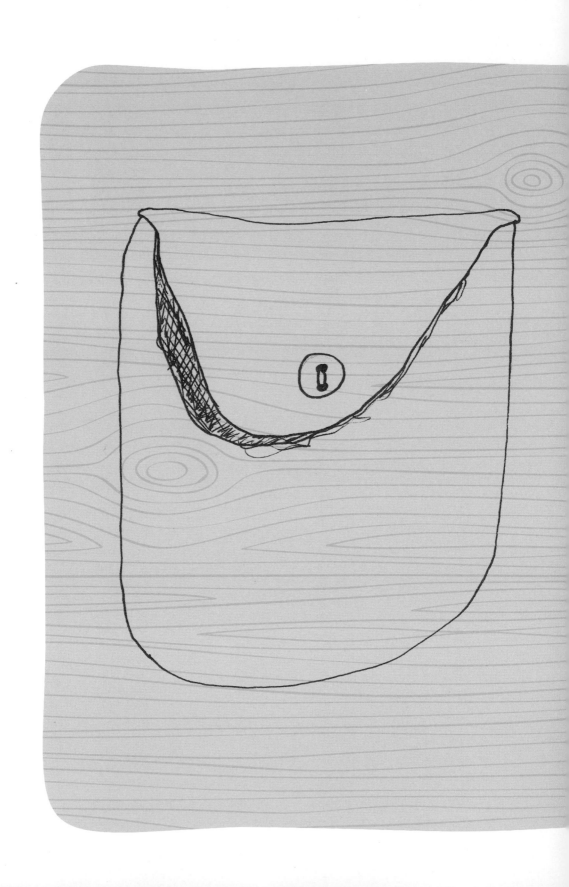

MAKE FELTED MATERIAL FROM NATURAL FIBERS

Felting is the process of taking raw animal fiber, most commonly wool, and rubbing it together, with the aid of a little hot water and soap, until the individual fibers interlock and shrink around each other to form a solid layer of material. Once you have worked the fibers into felt, they will not pull apart, and the edges do not fray. You can cut the felt in any shape you want, and it will hold its shape. You can felt clothing items in a three-dimensional shape, like a boot, all in one, without creating a flat material first and then cutting out and stitching the pieces together.

Felting is really not that difficult. While the name sounds like a bad conjugation of the verb "feel," the process really is about feeling. It's very tactile (all about touching), and when the intertwining fibers begin to lock together, the feeling of the fibers changes as you work your hands over them. The transition you feel is the indication that the individual fibers will, indeed, come together to create a unified piece of felt—and that feels good!

Although you are in constant motion and often vigorously rubbing the fibers you want to felt, this activity is very relaxing. It is also a process that you can stop any time, coming back in moments, hours, months, or years with no harm done. Felting is also an easy activity to do in the outdoors.

DISCOVERING FELT

Years ago, I saw this fellow sitting on the bank of the river with a big burlap bag of fiber and a dripping pile of wet wool in his hand. Being curious, I walked over and asked him what he was doing. He said he was felting, making a hat. Hmmm. I thought felt only came in primary colors, very thin, sold at the Five and Dime store in one-foot squares, and was only used by people who needed to cut a circle and glue it to the bottom of their child's pottery project so it wouldn't scratch the dining room dish cabinet.

I sunk my hands into the big bag of wool and Jack Fee said, "What do you want to make?" That was the beginning of my felting addiction.

I had been teaching ancestral skills, outdoor living, and survival skills for quite a few years, and in my business, Earth Knack, I focused on teaching classes that addressed Stone Age living skills. Although I did not consider felting a Stone Age cloth-making technology, I loved it, but I never could justify teaching felting classes at Earth Knack.

FELT IN HISTORY

I was painting the time line of human history along the top of the wall of our little museum at the Earth Knack school site, and a friend who had recently done some felting with me came running in and said, "Check this out!" He handed me a copy of *Discover* magazine. There was this big article with these incredible pictures of an archaeological dig of a burial site in the northwest China desert.

The buzz in the scientific community was that these mummies had Caucasian features, and they were buried with many objects that at the time of their death, over 5,000 years ago, had (supposedly) not yet been discovered in China. A small replica of a cart with a wheel, like a toy, was with one of the bodies. Some of the tools showed knowledge of metallurgy. The main focus of this article was that China had always claimed that its culture was not influenced by other cultures, and that all of its current technology and know-how had developed in-house, so to speak.

Here's the kicker: The foldout center picture of the magazine showed five of these mummified bodies with their artifacts and accouterments. My eyes popped wide open when I saw that they were dressed in thigh-high felted boots, felted vests, and wonderful tall, pointy felted hats! The felted clothes were brilliant red, blue, and yellow, perfectly preserved. (So maybe felt was supposed to come in primary colors!) The article said the bodies were at least 5,000 years old. That meant that felting *was* a Stone Age technology—imagine my excitement! I ran right to my calendar and listed a felting class on the Earth Knack class schedule for the coming month.

USES FOR FELT

You can felt bags, boots, vests, slippers, hats, and even shelter walls (think yurt). You can make practical items, like hot mitts or pads for the kitchen, or whimsical ones, like three-dimensional animal and fairy figures. Just about any form you could imagine sculpting with clay, you can create with raw animal and plant fibers using the felting method.

KNOWLEDGE

FIBER TYPES

Animal fibers felt best. You can add all kinds of plant fibers into your animal fiber material, but most of them don't felt very well. Many kinds of wool from sheep, llama, and alpaca felt beautifully. Cat hair felts okay when you mix it in with other fibers, but cats make me sneeze, so I don't use cat hair.

Lots of kinds of dog hair work well, but when you're in the water-and-soap stage of creating the felted material, you are surrounded by the odor of wet dog. It's an odiferous experience to stand in the rain with your dog-hair hat, and you'll notice that nobody stands next to you either. You will just have to experiment with the things that you would like to see what works for you.

While hiking through the Rocky Mountains, I have found a bit of mountain goat and wild sheep fiber caught up in willow branches or tangled up in tall grasses. It felts beautifully. So while you're out romping around in the woods, keep your eyes open for fiber. You never know what you're going to find out there.

Don't forget people hair! I have a friend we all call Santa. (He gets that name because he really could be Santa's twin brother.) For one full year, he brushed out his beautiful white hair and saved whatever he got in his hairbrush, putting it into a cloth bag. He brought this bag of his own hair to me, and together we made him a wonderful felted hat. My hair doesn't felt well. Maybe yours does.

MAKE A SAMPLE PATCH

Decide what kind of fiber you want to make something out of, and then collect a little bit of it for a sample felt patch to see how well the fiber shrinks and locks together. Not all fibers felt well, and not all fibers feel good against the skin. Try out the patch you make on your forearm or behind your knee, where your skin is very sensitive, before you make a whole article of clothing.

Get a small handful of the fiber you want to use. Gently pull and pick it apart so that all the individual fibers are fluffed up and out and elongated and the whole handful has at least doubled in size.

➡

KNOWLEDGE

In order to lock up and shrink well, a fiber needs several things.

1. It helps if the fiber has **kink**, or **crimp**. That means exactly what it sounds like. When you hold the individual fiber up in the air, is it absolutely straight or is it all kinky? If a fiber has kink, it is generally a good felting fiber. You can mix kinky fibers with straight ones to help them felt into your material better

2. Fibers also need a good **staple**. That means that they have enough length to twist and lock into other fibers around them. Fibers that are cut very short, or sheared off the animal very close to the hide, don't usually felt as well as longer fibers. So when you overhear someone say, "This is kinky! Is it staple?" it might make sense if they are preparing fiber for felting.

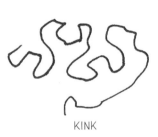

KINK

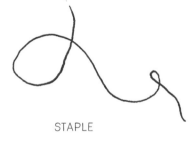

STAPLE

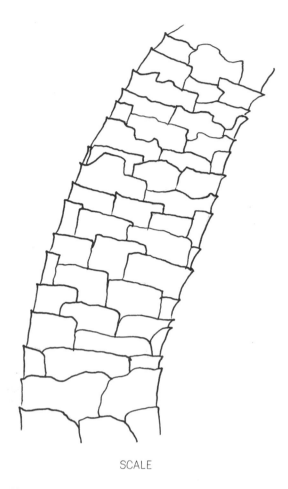

SCALE

3. Another important quality of a felting fiber is that it has **scale**. Scale is the character of a fiber that you really can't see unless you have a microscope. It means that all around the exterior of the fiber there are a bunch of little scales, just like a fish. These scales on the fiber allow it to grip and lock into the fibers around it. So, if your fiber has kink, staple, and scale, you have a good felting fiber

Because you can't see the scale on an individual fiber, it's not easy to tell whether the fiber you want to use is going to work well if you don't have any experience with the particular fiber or you haven't talked to anyone who's made a good piece of felt from it. Some fibers have long staple and good kink, but no scale, and some rather straight fibers have enough scale to actually felt well.

LAY UP THE FIBERS

Pull out a little bit of fiber from the big, fluffy cloud of fiber. Pull all the fibers in that one little bit until they are all lying in a similar direction. Lay the fiber down flat, perhaps on a dinner plate. Grab another little bit, and pull out the fibers so that they are lying in the same direction. Lay this bit of fiber at an angle on top of the first bit. The fibers below should not line up with the ones you are putting on now. Do this over and over, stacking layers of fiber at randomly opposing angles. Don't press down on the pile yet. Let it build up tall and fluffy with fibers going in all directions; that is what "lay up" means.

HEAT WATER

Make the water as hot as you can stand it. Now, put a drop of dish soap in your hands, and rub your palms and fingers so that they are coated in a thin layer of the dish soap. Next, fill a large glass or pitcher with hot water.

SET IN THE FIBERS

Gently dribble the hot water over the pile of fibers, letting the weight of the water flatten the fibers. Use your soapy fingertips, one at a time like you're typing on a keyboard, to gently tap down the fibers once they are dampened; that is what "set in" means.

➡

KNOWLEDGE

The soap prevents the fibers from sticking to your fingers. Without soap, the fibers would just lift up onto your fingers as you tap them, pulling them apart from one another instead of helping them stick together. Throughout this process, you will periodically need to re-soap your fingers and palms. If fibers start to catch on your fingers as you rub, apply the tiniest drop of soap. If you use too much soap, you'll have a lathery mess of loose fibers and the felting process will be prohibited. The hot water helps the fibers shrink.

IMPORTANT

Remember, you are dribbling just enough hot water to get the fibers to sink down and set into each other in a flat, wet layer. If you pour too much water, the fibers will float and separate from each other instead of shrinking together. If you pour too much water by accident, gently hold down the wet fibers with your soapy palm, and tip the plate to drain off the excess water.

FINGERTIPPING THE FIBERS

Once you have "set in" the fibers, letting the water settle them flat while you gently tapped your finger tips down to help the flattening, use those soapy fingertips to tap-tap-tap-tap the top of the fiber. Jack calls this "fingertipping." Just use your fingertips, setting in the fibers so that they flatten into a mat and start to grip each other. This is actually beginning to felt the fibers, but you will have to do this finger-tipping method for a while before the fibers hold together enough for you to start rubbing back and forth.

STARTING TO RUB

When you have fingertipped the fibers down so that the top layer of fibers has begun to grip into itself enough to withstand the light pres-sure of rubbing, you can slowly and very lightly begin to rub the top of the forming fiber patch with the flat bottom of your fingers and palms back and forth on the plate. Keep your hands very flat. Although it is very tempting, you never want to rub in circles. If you see and feel the fibers pulling apart under your fingers, you have started rubbing too soon; immediately return to fingertipping

KNOWLEDGE

When you rub in circles, you pull the fibers apart. Only move your hands in a back and forth direction, diagonally, or sideways—not in circles.

I'm not sure what it is about the rubbing in circles thing—everybody does it. I guess it's rather mindless and methodical, and when you've been rubbing for a while, you zone out. It's great to sing and dance and laugh when you felt, and certainly, just like the old quilting bees, a lot of talking goes on around the felting table. But if you don't stay focused, consciously rubbing back and forth, and find yourself tempted to the circle side, your fibers won't lock together and you won't make felt.

TECHNIQUE

When you first start rubbing back and forth, make your touch light as a feather. Go back and forth, side to side, or diagonally, but go lightly, almost as if you don't want the fibers to feel your hand. On a small patch like this, you can begin applying a little more pressure in just a minute or two. Staying focused will help you notice immediately if you're pressing too hard as you rub; you will feel the fibers separating from each other instead of gripping. If this is happening, immediately go back to fingertipping for a moment before returning to a lighter rubbing.

SKINNING UP

After a while, you will feel a tightening or a toughening of the top layer of fibers. I call this the "skinning up" stage. It's as if the patch is creating a tough outer skin. When you feel this, you know you're getting somewhere. It's a happy moment, especially if you're doing a big project like a pair of three-dimensional boots or a suit coat. Jack actually made a suit coat with lapels and everything—stylin'! Once the top layer has skinned up, you will be able to flip the whole pancake of fiber over.

FLIP THE FIBER OVER

It's an easy mistake to start rubbing the other side with as much pressure as you've been rubbing the first side. You haven't worked these fibers at all, so calm down a little and start with the fingertipping. Because it has been sitting at the bottom of the plate in the water, the fibers may be floating apart more than gripping together. Once you get started, however, this side will skin up much more quickly. Fingertip the fibers, then lightly rub back and forth in all directions, and when you feel the fibers begin to skin up, you can lift the whole pancake into your hands and rub both sides at once.

RINSING THE SOAP

If you have too much soap, the fibers will not stick together. When this happens to me, I gently place my palm over the fiber to hold it down, pour hot water to rinse the soap away, swirl it around a little, and tip up the plate to drain it. Sometimes I have to do this several times. The hot water rinse helps the fibers to shrink, but if they aren't gripping together well enough yet, the water can also make them come apart. Slow and gentle felts the fiber; enjoy the process. After rinsing, you usually still have to go back to applying a little bit of soap on your fingertips, but once you've overdone it a few times, you get much more cautious with the soap.

WORK THE PATCH ON BOTH SIDES

When you've gotten to the point that you can lift the whole piece and rub it on both sides between your palms, rinsing it in hot water won't be any problem. You can rub hard and vigorously, and you'll see the shrinking happening very quickly.

IMPORTANT

A very cool thing about the way fibers shrink when you are felting is that they shrink in the direction that you are rubbing. This is very helpful to know when you are making a hat or vest or boots and trying to get them to conform and fit to your body parts with a pleasing shape.

SHAPING THE FELT

You can play around with your sample patch, and as long as the fiber still has some room for shrinkage, you can turn the shape from a circle to a square to a triangle or whatever you want, simply by rubbing in the direction you want it to shrink. For example, if you have a circle, you can form it into a square by rubbing back and forth

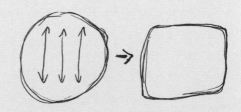

from one edge of the circle to the other, across the middle, and it will begin to shrink across those two opposite ends. Then, turn it 90 degrees and rub up and down that way. Those two edges will shrink towards each other. If you continue to do this only in those two directions, you'll see the four corners starting to form as your circle morphs into a square. You could rub back and forth vigorously in a line between the two diagonal corners and turn it back into a circle if you wanted.

MAKING NEAT EDGES

If you have very thin edges and you want to thicken them up, you can rub your fingertips back and forth on that little edge, pulling towards the center. If you have shrunk the fiber down as far as it will go but your edges are inconsistent (and you happen to care about that), you could take a pair of scissors and trim up your edges. It's a solid mat of fiber material, and it will not shred or fray.

KNOWLEDGE

All fiber has a shrinkage rate; different fibers shrink in different proportions. Even the same kind of fiber, say merino wool, will sometimes shrink at different rates from one animal to the next or one season to the next; sometimes there is a different shrinkage rate with fibers from the same animal. If you're making a larger project, it's good to make a test patch and see just how far down you can shrink the felt. If you're making boots and you want them to be thick, you'll want to plan your pattern large enough so that the fibers can shrink their full rate and the boots will still fit. If the project you are making is getting too small and the fiber hasn't finished shrinking, you can stop if you don't mind the felted material being thinner. If the project gets wet, hot, and agitated in the future, it will continue to shrink.

Now you know quite a bit about the characteristics of fiber, the kinds of fiber you can experiment with, and how to make a sample patch. If you like the process and want to do more, there is a lot of good information about felting patterns and projects already printed. You can find more good directions, as well as many kinds of fiber, at almost any yarn store.

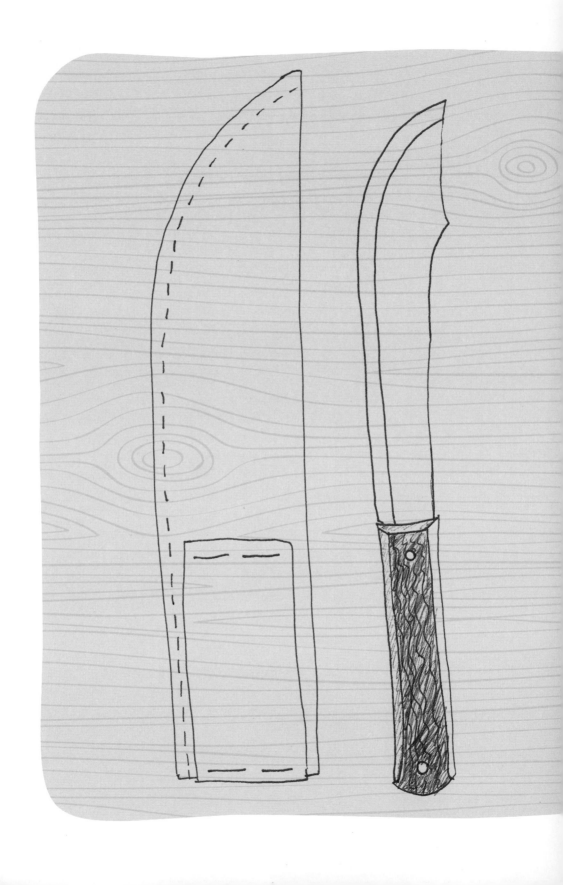

HOW AND WHY TO USE A METAL KNIFE IN THE WOODS

When I go play in the woods or take a wilderness or survival jaunt, my favorite knife to carry is an Old Hickory, a brand that's sold at most grocery stores across the country. They are often found hanging on little white plastic tabs in the aisles, packaged individually, in sizes from a paring knife to a lightweight cleaver.

WHY?

I go for the butcher knife with the six-inch blade, the hickory handle being about five inches long. They are simple, strong, durable, and best of all, whackable! At anywhere from twelve to sixteen dollars in cost (at present), using a hammer stone to drive them down into a deer leg is of no concern, and it's very effective. Splitting a branch to make a fire set (see Make a Matchless Campfire, p. 165) doesn't faze you or the knife. If you had just

spent a good amount of money on a fancy survival knife, you would be hesitant to use it in all the possible ways that a good woods knife is really needed to be used when you're kickin' about in nature.

BONUS

The blades of the Old Hickory knives are made with a lower-carbon steel than stainless steel. This is great news if you find a piece of flint and can strike the flint edge and steel together to make sparks.

But wait! There's more! They are really easy to sharpen. Yes, they also dull more quickly because the metal is softer, but if you have a fancy higher-carbon-content knife blade and have tried to get it back to its original edge after use, you don't need me to say any more.

No, I'm not taking a cut of sales from Old Hickory. Shucks! I have, however, carried their product for many years, being out in the wilderness in survival conditions for up to three and a half months at a time, and I have never had a reason to want any other knife. Enough said.

CONSIDER

No matter what kind of knife you have, it's really important to know how to use it properly. If you're depending on your knife and you break it, you might be really disappointed if you spent a lot of money on it, but that's not the real loss. The important part was that you were depending on it.

You've already learned how to make a stone knife (see Make a Stone Knife, p. 27). That's good. In fact, that's great! I have taught many courses over the years, from making a bow to butchering a buffalo using only stone tools. Yes, stone knives work, and they work well, but there is a feeling of security in having a metal sheath knife strapped to your hip, ready to do the slicing, carving, butchering, scraping, spark striking, and so many other things that need to be done on an active walk through the woods. Treat it well and keep track of it, and you'll have a great ally in the woods.

SOLID BLADE/TANG ASSEMBLY

I recommend a knife that is made all in one piece, as opposed to a folding or pocketknife. When the **blade**, or cutting end, and the **tang**, or handle end, are one length of metal, the knife has less parts to break. It has more blade length and handle weight, making it versatile in a survival situation; you can apply more pressure and torque to the blade; it's useful for bigger jobs; it's harder to lose; and you don't run the risk of catching your fingertips when you go to close it.

SHEATH YOUR KNIFE

When you keep your knife in a sheath, the cutting edge is covered, keeping your body parts safer and keeping the blade out of the dirt, which can dull the edge. A dull edge is not safe to use. (See Safe Handling of Tools and Knives, p. 39, for more on knife safety.) A sheath allows less exposure to moisture, which can rust the blade. A low-carbon steel blade rusts more quickly than a stainless steel blade. The benefits of a lower-carbon-content steel blade are worth the maintenance required.

KNIFE MAINTENANCE

If your blade gets rusty, rub it with steel wool or fine sand until the rust is gone, and then gently rub vegetable oil (or another cooking oil) into the metal. That usually takes care of it. If a folding knife rusts, it is much more difficult to clean up, and it is almost impossible to get the rust out of the crevices. If you are out on a survival jaunt and don't have any cooking oil, you can use the grease from fish skins or animal fat from some critter you snared, trapped, or hunted.

IMPORTANT NOTE

Remember this: You are not at the top of the food chain. Let me repeat that: *You are not at the top of the food chain.* Most of us have forgotten this, and it is a part of that lower level of awareness that we, as modern people, have compared to our ancestors. When you're out in the woods, day or night, it's a good thing to remember that you are just one part of the big picture. Being thoughtful about fishing, how you dispose of fish entrails, what kind of smells you get all over your clothes, and how clean you keep your campsite are not only important considerations but also, sometimes, matters of survival.

♦♦ SHARPENING YOUR KNIFE

It's a good idea to carry a small sharpening stone with you. Some sheaths have a small pocket on the outside for a sharpening stone. If you're out in the woods and you don't have a manufactured sharpening stone, you can actually sharpen your knife with a fine-grained rock that you find lying around; this works especially well for a low-carbon steel blade.

Get yourself a basic sharpening stone with a fine side and a coarse side. You can find these almost anywhere sporting goods are sold, and most of them come in a little package with a set of directions. Practice. If you don't get your knife very sharp and you go to use it, you'll find out quickly that you need to sharpen it some more. When I am butchering an elk, I generally have three or four knives ready to go, and I sharpen them several times before all the meat is finally in canning jars lining the root-cellar shelves. When you use a knife, sharpening it is a constant activity.

There are many books and instructional videos on how to sharpen your knife (see Resources, p. 302). Most of them are quite useful. Some get mired down in technical terms and a rigid procedure to achieve the ultimate sharp edge. This thoroughly accurate approach can make knife sharpening rather inaccessible.

ALWAYS CARRY YOUR KNIFE

Figure out a way to comfortably carry your knife around with you. If you feel comfortable carrying it with you, you will always have it when you need it. A knife lying on the dresser at home, or tucked into the kitchen drawer, is useless when you need one in the woods. When someone asks my friend Darry Wood if he has a knife on him, he always responds with the question, "Do I have my pants on?" Fortunately, I've never seen him without his knife!

USING THE EDGE

When you're skinning an animal, cutting meat, or opening a fish, let the sharp edge of your blade do the work. Don't force the knife blade in and through things. Draw the blade gently, almost as if you were softly petting a cat, and allow the thin edge to cut. Come back over this area several times if you need to. Your knife will stay sharper, your fingers will stay safer, and you will not waste energy if you don't go hacking about the job.

TECHNIQUE

If you're cutting through a thick stick or piece of wood, begin by cutting a notch into the wood or branch from either side, pressing the knife away from you at an angle, first in one direction, then in another. It is the same method you use to swing a hatchet into the trunk of a tree: first some downward cuts and then some upward cuts, letting the blade chip away layers and making a triangular wedge shape as you progress. This is quick, efficient, effective, and much less frustrating than trying to hack your way straight through or saw with a sharp edge that is not designed for sawing.

FIND YOUR WAY WITH THE MOON AND STARS

The path that the sun and moon appear to take through the sky is a wide band that sky watchers have named the ecliptic belt. Standing here on Earth, we see the sun, the moon, and the twelve major constellations that make up what is called the zodiac move along this belt. If we could take a great big piece of white chalk and draw the two outer edges of this pathway or belt on the sky, the space in between would be about sixteen degrees. Not only do the zodiac constellations, the sun, and the moon appear to rise, travel, and set within the boundaries of that belt, but over an eighteen-year period, the moon moves from one side of the belt to the other.

HISTORY

There are many locations on the planet that have evidence of ancient sky watchers tracking the patterns and movement of the sun. There are fewer discovered locations that demonstrate ancestral knowledge of the moon's thirty-six-year journey across the ecliptic belt and back again. Chaco Canyon, located in the Chaco Culture National Historical Park (a UNESCO World Heritage site), in northern New Mexico is one of these places. The Four Corners School of Outdoor Education collaborates with the American Museum of Natural History to offer courses in Chaco Canyon. I have had the opportunity to teach there several times, bringing ancestral-living skills into the course curriculum. If you haven't had the opportunity to get there—go!

CONSIDER

In How and Why to Use a Metal Knife in the Woods, p. 131, we talked about the level of observation and awareness our ancestors practiced. If you're still holding on to the concept that ancestral people were "primitive," look into the available information on the age of some of these lunar (moon) tracking sites. Then think about the fact that it takes eighteen years for the moon to move across the ecliptic belt one way, and a total of thirty-six years for it to move from one edge of the belt across and back again. So perhaps in one person's lifetime (and remember lifetimes weren't as long back then as they are now), the observation of this thirty-six-year cycle could be made if someone happened to pay close attention.

IMAGINE

Because you've seen a thing happen one time in one particular way doesn't guarantee you'll ever see it again. So just try to imagine how many thirty-six-year cycles it would've taken for people to begin to feel relatively sure they were watching a repeating pattern. The artwork inscribed in stone and the large lithic (stone) constructions we have found that mark and predict this moon movement pattern represent advanced analytic thinking, and they required huge amounts of effort, persistence, and energy to create. A lot of observation, awareness, high-level thinking, and oral storytelling went into mapping the movement of heavenly bodies.

INSPIRATION

Do you suppose it's just a coincidence that so many of these maps were created in stone? After all, any material could have been used, and perhaps many maps were made out of materials that quickly or slowly degraded and are no longer seen. I believe that a lot of information was passed down to us in the lithic record by ancestors who valued knowledge and knew that our well-being would depend on the knowledge they had worked so long and hard to acquire. Over great spans of time, the knowledge written in stone was the knowledge that would remain intact. The stories of oral tradition would shift and change with the teller and the times, and articles of clothing or tools would break, disintegrate, and recycle back into the earth.

KNOWLEDGE

The moon moves up and over us along a path that shifts from a southerly area of the sky to a more northerly area of the sky over an eighteen-year period. The sun also moves from the southern edge of the belt (in winter) to the northern edge of the belt (in summer), but unlike the moon, the sun does this over the course of four seasons, not eighteen years.

TRACK MOON AND SUN SHADOWS

TRY THIS AT HOME

On the walls of the house, I have recorded the rising place of the moon and the sun over the last twenty years here at Earth Knack. In your area, if you're paying attention and you keep track of things a little bit, this information can help you get a better sense of north and south, depending on the season and the year. Becoming confident about directions is very valuable.

WINTER SHADOWS

In the last part of December, around midday when the sun is shining, you can stick a stick in the ground and immediately get a shadow that runs from the base of your stick in a northerly direction. This time of year, the sun is on that southern edge of the ecliptic belt, and it will always cast a shadow towards the north.

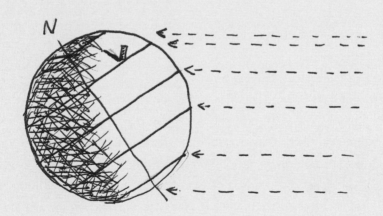

KNOWLEDGE

The stars also offer good directional information to those roaming about at night. Most people are familiar with the twelve constellations that are found within the sixteen-degree width of the ecliptic belt. Their names are also known as the twelve signs of the zodiac. We use these names for the birthday sign we were born under. You may have heard it in the infamous pickup line: "Hey, baby! What's your sign?"

LEARN TO RECOGNIZE THE CONSTELLATIONS

Starting the list with the winter solstice (which is the longest night and shortest day in the northern hemisphere, falling on December 21 or 22, because the northern part of Earth has tipped away from the sun as it spins around that life-giving star, giving us less light each day), the constellations are: Capricorn, Aquarius, Pisces, Aries, Taurus, Gemini, Cancer, Leo, Virgo, Libra, Scorpio, and Sagittarius.

Once you learn their patterns and how to recognize them in the sky, you will find these constellations within the confines of the ecliptic belt. They are most prevalent in the night sky during the months that they are associated with. For example, Capricorn dominates the mid-December night sky.

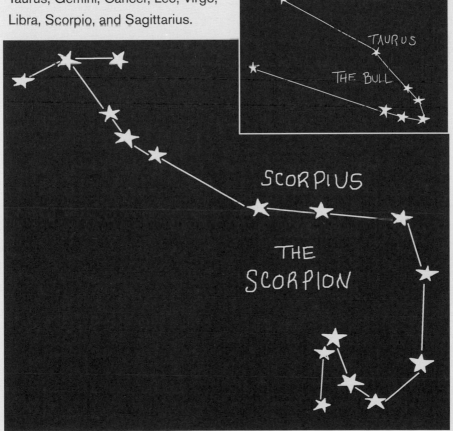

Remember, these constellations appear to rise and set just like the moon and sun. If you can find the constellation and watch it move through the night, you can determine east and west. This navigational trick would be helpful when the moon isn't out, shining too brightly, which makes it harder to see the stars.

LEARN TWO MORE CONSTELLATIONS

Learn to recognize the Big Dipper and Orion constellations. While Orion will appear to rise in the east and set in the west and help you identify an east-west direction, the Big Dipper will not. The Big Dipper is one of several constellations we call circumpolar, which means that it goes in a circle around the North Pole. Because most of us can recognize the Big Dipper, it's worth talking about how it moves in the sky. Being a circumpolar constellation, the Big Dipper makes a circle around the place in the sky that we call true north. A little point of light marks that place in the sky, and we call it the North Star.

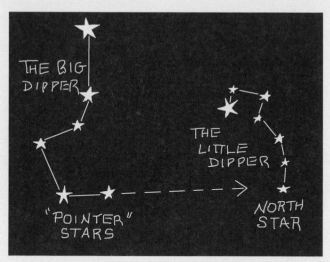

QUESTION
Why do we call the North Star's location "true north"?

ANSWER
Our beautiful little Earth is spinning round and round like a toy top. Imagine that

spinning toy and the handle and tip sticking out of each end. Pretend the handle and tip are Earth's South Pole and North Pole. Earth's pole is its axis, an imaginary centerline that it spins around. If you took a marker and drew a line from the South Pole to the North Pole and then kept going straight on up forever into space, somewhere way out there and far away along the line would be that little star that we call the North Star. We call it the North Star because it is in line with our North Pole. (The North Star is also called the pole star.) It doesn't get any more north than that, and so we call that place true north.

The Big Dipper **circles** around the North Star, which marks the spot where our North Pole would extend out into space. That's why we call the Big Dipper a **circumpolar** constellation. (Circum is a Latin word meaning "around.") A cool thing to know is that Polaris, the star we call the North Star today, has not always been our pole star. The earth wobbles on its axis over time, and many thousands of years ago, its pole was in line with a different star.

So, you recognize the Big Dipper constellation; you know it is going to circle around the North Star; and you know it will be visible to you most of the night. If you keep an eye on it, you won't have any trouble figuring out which way north is! See why it was worth explaining?

My favorite star book is *The Stars* by H.A. Ray (yes, the *Curious George* author). It was first written in 1952, and it's still accurate because the earth hasn't wobbled too much since then.

♠♠
DRAW THE BIG DIPPER

Draw a line connecting the stars of the Big Dipper to make the dipper shape. (It's called the Big Dipper because it looks like a cup with a large curved handle for dipping out water.) The side of the cup farthest from the handle has two stars. Draw a line between these two stars, starting at the bottom of the cup; this line points to the North Star. Keep drawing the line straight out into space, and you will end up at the North Star. That's why we call these two stars the pointer stars!

MAKE YOUR OWN PAINTS WITH EARTH MINERALS

Pigment is the color that can be taken out of sandy soil, clay, or rock to make paints or stains. Any time you find earth minerals in almost any form, you can prepare them and test them to see if you can get a good paint or stain. Stains can also be made from plant materials by extracting the pigment from the tissues and cells. Sometimes paints and stains are easy to make in a water solution; sometimes oil or fat makes a better base.

Good news, homeschoolers! Working with earth mineral paints and stains is a wonderful activity for the elementary or early middle school science curriculum.

MAKE PIGMENT PAINTS AND DYES

COLLECT MATERIALS

The first thing to do is wander about in the woods, over hill and dale, or just keep a lookout from the car window, and when you see a pretty colored earth that you like, collect up a little bit in a small paper lunch bag or a clean peanut butter jar.

PREPARE THE MATERIALS

If what you pick up is hard and rocky, you'll want to crush it down into a powder between two stones. If the colored earth you collect is like clay and is all dried out, you'll pulverize it into powder as well. If it's all wet and mucky, scoop the earth into a little plastic bucket or a jar, and leave it that way until you're ready to prepare the paint or stain. The color you like might be in a soil that is grainy or sandy; it's possible that you can use it just the way it is, or you might have to grind it down more to get the pigment out.

TEST FOR COLOR CONTENT

When you get your colorful earth home, test it for pigment content by mixing it up with just enough water to make it pourable, and then

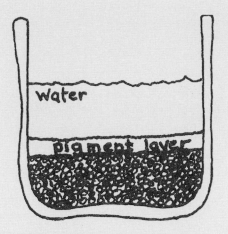

water

pigment layer

pour it into a clear glass jar that is tall and thin. What happens next is that the soil content, the pigment content, and the water content separate into layers. Because the glass jar is clear, you can see these layers form. Some of your soils and rocks will create a nice fat pigment layer, but some of the pigment layers will be really thin. If you really like the colors from the soils that have a very thin pigment layer, you will need a lot of soil to get enough pigment to do a project of any size.

SEPARATE THE COLOR FROM THE WATER

Once you've tested the soil in a glass jar and prepared more earth for the color you like, you'll want a large bowl or bucket with a wide opening to pour in the mixed earth and water. The larger opening will make it easier to pour off the

water after the layers separate and scrape the soft pigment layer off the harder grainy soil below. If the soft pigment layer is wet enough, you can use it as paint immediately. When it dries out, you can simply add a little more water to make it paintable again.

USES

Paints like this work well on projects you make out of rawhide, on the walls of your home (especially when the walls are a handmade adobe plaster like the ones here in our little hogan), or on pottery projects you're getting ready to fire.

MAKE A CRAYON INSTEAD

If you don't want to paint on things and would rather make more of a crayon, sort of like a grease pencil, you can let the soft, moist pigment layer dry out in a bowl. Press the

➡

pigment with your finger until it crumbles into powder, and then add some kind of tallow that stays hard at room temperature. Tallow is rendered animal fat (see Make a Lamp and Candles, p. 231). I use deer and elk fat for making pigment crayons. Bear grease doesn't work for making crayons because it is liquid at room temperature, but it's great for face and body paint or making handprints and other designs on your pony!

MORE USES

You can also use pigments mixed with tallow to make designs on leather clothing or shoes. These tallow crayons work well on canvas, muslin, and other natural fiber cloth like cotton or linen or hemp. If you make a yurt or tepee liner out of canvas, earth mineral pigment paints are a wonderful way to decorate your cloth walls. Use the plant syrup discussed below to make your pigment paints more waterproof.

WATERPROOF THE PAINT

Certain plants can make a fixative, a syrupy waterproofing substance that you add to your pigments for exterior walls or things you use outside. Prickly pear, cottonwood buds, and gumweed can all be put in a big metal pot and boiled down to a thick syrup. Add enough water

to cover the plant material. As the mixture boils, add more water so the pot bottom doesn't scorch. Stir until the liquid is a thick syrup. Then just mix the pigments you collect with this syrup instead of water. You can also use the pigments first and paint the syrup over the finished painting. I used this fixative on the outside walls of my home.

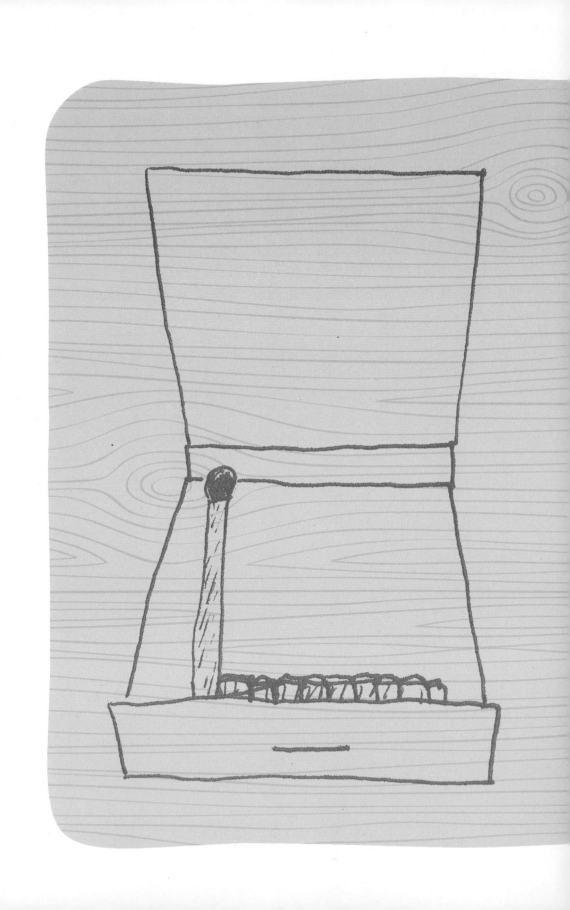

LIGHT A ONE-MATCH CAMPFIRE

Most folks just can't wait to start a campfire. That is precisely why most of us don't get the campfire lit the first time we try. In campgrounds and fire pits across the land, a one-match fire is a rare thing, even in dry conditions. Skillful campfire making takes preparation and practice.

♠♠
MAKE A ONE-MATCH FIRE

Following these simple steps will ensure that your campfire starts easily every time. Before you even look for your matches, collect your kindling or tinder. You want to collect at least two big handfuls of kindling that are no thicker than the matchstick you use to light the fire. If you have ever tried lighting a campfire before, you already know that you would not strike the match and hold it under a full-size log, hoping for the fire to light. You want to patiently work your way up in size, starting with very thin sticks. When your matchstick-sized sticks have caught fire, add sticks that are just a bit thicker, letting them catch fire before adding more sticks that are just a bit thicker. Continue adding sticks of increasing size and letting them catch fire, and finally, you will be able to place that log and have it burn.

COLLECT KINDLING PIECES
Search for kindling sticks that are at least 4 or 5 inches long. If your kindling sticks are too short, it will be hard to layer them up so they will support each other. If the pile of kindling you make doesn't hold its structure, you'll have a much more difficult time getting your fire started. Of course, you want to find the driest possible kindling you can.

SPLIT KINDLING PIECES

If you are in a very wet area, you can split sticks into many slivered pieces to make good kindling. Even if they are wet on the outside, they will often be dry on the inside. Slivered pieces of bark can make good kindling if there aren't many sticks, and dried grasses, the woody stems of dried-out plants, and pine needles can often be good additions to your kindling pile.

Once you collect those first two big handfuls of very thin kindling sticks, set them in a pile close to where you will start your fire. Now go get two big handfuls of kindling sticks that are just a little bit thicker than the first pile. Set those in a separate pile next to the first pile of kindling. Now go get two more big handfuls of sticks thicker than the second pile. Set this third pile next to the second.

Nope, don't go get your matches yet! Go get two more handfuls about as thick as your thumb. Lay those down in line with the rest. Then go get sticks that are the width of two fingers; get a small armload of those. You know where to put them. Off you go again for wrist-size sticks, gathering another small armload. And finally, go gather an armload of ankle-size sticks.

HOW TO BUILD UP THE KINDLING

How you pile up your first small kindling sticks makes a difference to how well you will be able to catch them on fire. Layer the first pieces of kindling in a tall pile, or lean them up against each other in a cone or teepee shape. Either way, as you carefully place your kindling, make a small opening at the bottom where you can insert your burning match. If this opening is too small, the kindling sticks will snuff out the flame when you go to push the match in.

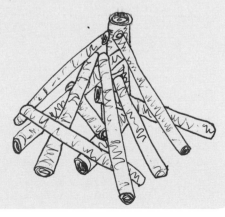

KNOWLEDGE

In order to create fire, you need three things: **fuel** (kindling), **heat** (provided by the combustion of the sulfur tip on your matches), and **air** (oxygen). If you tightly clump up all of your smallest kindling sticks, it is difficult for the oxygen to assist the combusting match head. If you place each piece of kindling too far apart, there won't be enough fuel for the small flame to catch.

If you try to light the kindling from the side or the top, you are not taking advantage of the fact that heat rises. Because heat rises, people often strike a match and hold the sulfur tip upwards so that their fingers don't burn. If you do this when you are trying to make a one-match fire, you will probably have to strike a second match. A match held vertically goes out very quickly because there is no fuel. You need to let the flame burn the matchstick. If the matchstick isn't actually on fire before you try to light the kindling, it will probably go out.

TECHNIQUE

Be patient and move slowly. If you quickly put the match to the bottom of the kindling pile, it's almost like blowing it out. You are moving the match through the air so fast that the air puts the flame out. Hold the matchstick horizontally, with the tip just slightly downward. Don't be afraid of burning your fingers. If you have chosen your kindling well and built your pile up as described, you will have enough time for your kindling to catch fire before your fingers feel the heat.

PRACTICE STRIKING MATCHES

It might sound silly, but one way to practice is by striking some matches. Most of us don't have a good reason to use matches much anymore, so you probably need some practice anyway. Get yourself a box of wooden matches and a safe container to drop burnt matchsticks into. Now just strike a bunch of them. Making a good strike takes a particular finesse, let alone not dropping it as soon as it flames up because you're afraid you will get burned. Strike a bunch and see how they burn, what angle is best, and how long they burn. You can make a matchstick burn a little longer if you tip it upward once the stick is fully in flame. You'll have to tip it back down again fairly quickly because the burnt charcoal won't stay in flames for long, but if you tip it back and forth, you'll get more burning time.

ROLE MODEL

People tell children not to play with matches. This usually means "Don't touch the matches!" Matches, like all tools, are not toys and should not be trifled with; rather, they should be used properly and often. Helping our children become capable and versatile, as opposed to denying them access to things we consider dangerous, is actually the very thing that keeps them safe.

LIGHT KINDLING WITH A MATCH

Before you strike the match, have your second pile of kindling close at hand. As soon as your first sticks begin to catch fire, you will carefully layer the next sticks above and around those catching fire. If you just toss them on top, you might collapse your pile, and the flames will go out. As those second sticks begin to catch fire, gently layer up your third pile. Now you're ready to lean your thumb-size sticks all around the outside of your pile of burning kindling.

The kindling is lit! Good job! Don't go anywhere yet; stay put and add your two-finger-wide sticks. Then add your wrist-size sticks. Finally, put your ankle-size sticks in place around the burning pile. At this point, you can be pretty certain that your fire is established. Now if you want to go running around the woods looking for more fuel and larger logs, you have some time to do that without your kindling pile burning up and going out before you return. Remember not to wander too far, and always be able to keep your eye on the fire as you collect more fuel.

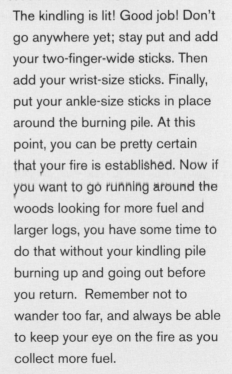

LIGHT KINDLING WITH A LIGHTER

Maybe you don't use matches. If you are going to use a butane lighter, it's pretty easy to overheat your thumb while holding the lighter under the kindling pile. Take about three of your matchstick-size pieces of kindling, hold them out horizontally, and light their tips on fire with your lighter. If the tips are just slightly spread apart, they will provide fuel for each other and retain their flames as you place them in the opening you made in your kindling pile.

Sometimes you find yourself in an area where there are only bigger logs, and kindling and/or smaller wood is difficult to find. Take that Old Hickory knife out of the sheath and split off several thin slats from the edge of a larger piece of wood. Split some of those slats into long, thin strips for kindling. Increasing the surface area of each strip of wood can really help your fire get going. Take your knife and gently hack down the edges of each split, making little hatch marks all over. This creates more fuel, allowing the flame to heat those little hacked bits and curls of wood and assist the combustion of the kindling.

MAKE PITCH POWDER

If you can find some pitch (see How to Make a Drum, p. 89), you can grind it between two stones, and then sprinkle the powdery pitch all over your kindling pile. It doesn't really create a solid flame, but it assists in a quicker heat up and creates little flares that can help substandard kindling catch fire more easily.

Besides, ground pitch is a really fun (and safe) way to add excitement to your campfires. Grind up a few handfuls, and once your flames are going well, toss a little pitch powder into the center of the fire! It's all snap, sparkle, pop, and pretty spits of color, without any of the dangers of fireworks, gunpowder, or gasoline.

SAFETY

Too many horror stories are told of people who resort to explosive fire-starting methods. Don't be one of those stories.

Good fire maintenance is a skill all of its own. The person who tends the fire, known as the fire tender, is a well-appreciated member of the campfire circle. Once the campfire is started, the magic usually begins. Stories get told, songs get sung, the tall tales get taller, the logs turn to embers, and the embers to ash. A good fire tender is paying attention. Ready with a good fire poker, the tender prods and pushes the burning logs into the center of the fire, getting the unburned ends into the coals and allowing them to flame up. This rotation of the logs reduces smoke and maintains light and warmth. The tender is ready to add logs as needed and has made sure there is a good stash of firewood just outside the campfire circle. All eyes and ears are on the storytellers, but in the end, the hero, although often unsung, is the mindful fire tender.

ROLE MODEL

Happy and successful outdoor living requires campers who live by the motto: "see a need, fill a need." On all expeditions, great or small, it is those who keep the water jugs full, a pot boiling, the firewood pile full, and the essential camp gear clean and organized who truly determine the success of the outing.

Part of good fire maintenance is stacking up a nice woodpile. If you are in an area where your fire pit will be used again by other campers, collecting a little more wood than you need that you can leave behind when you go, is always a happy welcome to the newcomers.

SAFETY

Stack your woodpile away from the main fire circle so that sparks and burning embers won't catch your pile on fire. Keeping the woodpile away from the fire also ensures that you won't be tripping over loose sticks and branches as you move around the fire, especially once it is dark. As you walk toward a burning flame at night, it is hard to see what's on the ground around you. Stumps left out as seats, personal camp gear or dishes left on the ground, and especially a spread out woodpile can create a tripping disaster. Additionally, if you are using the fire to cook on, you are usually more focused on your cooking activity and less on what is lying about on the ground around your feet. Nobody wants the camp cook to sprawl head over heels into the dirt or the burning coals while preparing the peach cobbler.

The burning embers, the flames, or a glowing pile of coal: we are fascinated and hypnotized. Mindlessly, while circling round the fire, people will often pick up a stick, set the end in the coals, let the stick catch on fire, and then whip the burning stick up and around in a happy-go-lucky tilt-a-whirl fashion. This is particularly fascinating at night when the glowing red stick end traces patterns in the dark, trailing a dragon tail of smoke. Flaming marshmallows incite this same stick-waving behavior. We're not just talking about kids here, folks! So few of us spend time around fire anymore, that we (adults and kids alike) forget its very real consequences. I have seen some gruesome fireside injuries over the years, and "Flaming Stick Tip Comes in Contact with Body Parts" is on the list. "Burning Marshmallow Catches Hair on Fire" is also on the list. Again, don't be that story.

KNOWLEDGE

There is an art to being a good campfire cook. Experience with campfires will teach you that coals and flames offer different levels of heat. Flames of different colors deliver more or less heat intensity. The kind of wood you burn and the conditions in which you are burning will determine the fire's temperature. Some woods pop and shoot lots of sparks. Some woods produce a lot of ash. Burning a certain kind of wood can guarantee you'll have some coals in the morning, while another kind can guarantee you'll spend all night long feeding the fire to maintain even the feeblest flame. Once you learn how the woods in your area work, your campfire cooking will improve.

▲▲ COOK ON THE FIRE

Once you know how to start up the campfire well and keep it safely maintained, it's a lot of fun to start cooking on it. From an environmental standpoint, you could reduce your use of manufactured fuels such as white gas, propane, butane, and kerosene. From another environmental standpoint, if you're in an area with very little dead or downed wood (wood already fallen to the ground), it would be good to consider alternatives to burning wood.

DISHES FOR FIRE COOKING

Be thoughtful about the dishes that you use on the coals. This may seem obvious, but be sure to choose pots, pans, lids, and utensils that do not have plastic parts. In these days of unusual material combinations and dishes for microwave use, not only is it hard to recognize plastic parts but it can also be hard to remember that they don't hold up to the heat of a campfire. Pots with lids will keep popping bits of charcoal and ash out of your boiling water and food, and pots with legs, although a little more difficult to find, make adding to or adjusting the heat of your coals or flames easier.

KNOWLEDGE

You can always set three or more stones of equal height in your coals and set your pot on these; however, the stones rob some of the heat from the pot. If you use the stones as a pot support and intend to use the coals afterwards for cooking anything directly on or in the coals, make sure you remove the rocks. Also, be thoughtful about what kind of rocks you heat up; some rocks crack or explode, sending sharp bits flying out and around the campfire. Generally these rocks come from areas around streams or riverbeds, but you will get to know the rock types in your area

TECHNIQUE

Working around a campfire can be a hot job. Get down low when you check under pot lids, test food baking on the coals, or add more wood to the fire. Reach in from around the lower edges of the fire pit. That way, you will not be leaning over the fire pit area, and the rising heat will not sear your skin. Place your cooking pots on the upwind side of the fire so that you will not have a constant wall of heat and a curtain of smoke in your face. You can cook better when you can breathe. You also look better after you are done cooking if you still have your eyebrows!

TIP

Tie a little length of light string or a piece of plant fiber to the top of a stick, and then set the stick upright in the ground along the edge of the fire pit. Throughout your camping trip, the wind will constantly shift. Setting up to prepare a meal will be easier if you know the general direction of the breeze before you build up your fire and place all your pots.

SAFETY

Flip-flops and shorts are not a good campfire cooking uniform. Popping coals can land anywhere, especially between the sole of your foot and the sole of your flip-flop, and hot food and water are likely to spill. Long pants and long-sleeved shirts, as well as closed-toe shoes, will make your cooking experience much more enjoyable, not to mention safe. When worn around the campfire, nylon, Lycra, and polypropylene clothing are a wax-museum nightmare waiting to happen. These materials melt and stick to skin, as one old Vietnam vet I used to work survival courses with would say, "Just like napalm!"

PUT THE FIRE "DEAD OUT"

When you are all done with your campfire, it can actually be rather tricky to put it completely out. The only sure way to know that you have really left your campfire area in a safe condition is to put your hands deep down into the area under where the campfire was and feel no heat; don't walk away until you can do this. A good way to help yourself put out the fire is to make sure you don't burn more wood than you need, but this can be difficult since everyone loves to throw wood on the fire. If it's getting late and everyone's getting tired, don't add any more wood to the fire. The fire tender can relax, and the final conversations can happen around the dying embers.

If you're trying to make a quick breakfast before you get on your way, gather up a lot of finger-width sticks instead of larger logs. As you cook, stay busy feeding the flames. You'll be able to put the fire out much more quickly if you don't have a lot of coals or large burning log ends. Try to burn your fire completely down to ash before you put it out.

USING WATER TO PUT OUT FIRE

If you have water to put out the fire, pour it on slowly and evenly, and use a big stick to stir the water into the ash. Stand upwind as you pour to avoid the plume of steam and ash that usually spurts out of the hot fire pit when you pour the water. Add water and continue to stir until there is no sizzle or steam. If you can place your hand in the center of the fire pit area and not feel any heat, your fire is "dead out," as the Forest Service signs say.

CONSIDER

There are forest fires that have started because heat traveled down from the bottom of the fire pit area and made contact with root material, coal, or other flammable substances in the ground, sometimes remaining undetected underground for hours, days, or even years! Then, at some point, the underground smoldering reaches the surface, finds oxygen, and combusts. Holy smokes! When you consider this possibility, although certainly a rare occurrence, you can't be too careful putting out your campfire.

USING DIRT TO PUT THE FIRE OUT

If you don't have water, you can still put out your campfire. Remember, fire needs oxygen and fuel, so your job is to remove the oxygen and the fuel. This is easier to do if you let the fire burn completely down to ash. Take a heavy stick and beat down any little pieces of remaining coal into dust. Then, use the stick to stir the fire pit area. Smash into powder any smoldering embers you see. Stir around all the hot spots, beating down any coals, smashing any embers, and releasing the heat from the ground area. Simply covering a hot fire pit area with a layer of sand or dirt is not enough to put it "dead out." Adding dirt or sand while stirring gets all the heat out. It's is a messy way to put out a fire, but it works.

RESEARCH CAMPFIRE ALTERNATIVES

There are some simple, small, lightweight stoves for camp cooking designed to burn small sticks and give great heat—a great choice for the environment, safety, easy use, and portability. They are also easy to mimic and build for yourself, even out of something as lightweight as a used 12-ounce soda can! There are lots of directions and designs for what's often called a soda-can rocket stove. The internet is a good resource for rocket stove technology. Outdoor stores often sell several models.

↟

RECYCLE YOUR CHARCOAL

Before you smash down all the bits of charcoal to put out the fire, remember that charcoal is a very useful resource when you are playing in the woods or relearning ancestral life skills. If you are spending a bit of time around a campfire, why buy charcoal at the supermarket if you are often making your own?

USES FOR CHARCOAL

You can save charcoal for backyard barbecuing or future Dutch oven campfire cooking, as described in Dutch Oven Cooking, p. 279. I use old ground charcoal from the fire pit as an effective rodent deterrent. Our Earth Knack blacksmith shop has old-time open forges. Early ranchers and homesteaders used wood charcoal in their forges when they didn't have coal. Wood charcoal burns less hot than coal but is perfectly effective for working metal, and even forge welding. The great forests of New England were logged out in our country's early years, not just for lumber to build but largely to supply the metal smelting industry with wood charcoal.

CHARCOAL AS PIGMENT

You can pick up a piece of charcoal and draw with it just like chalk. Decorate rocks out in the woods and the next rain will wash it away, offering a fresh canvas for your creativity. It's kind of like the Southwestern sand paintings, made for the current occasion and not meant to last.

MORE PERMANENT BLACK PIGMENT

You can crush your charcoal down and mix it with fat or oil. That way, the deep black pigment you make will spread evenly on many kinds of surfaces. You'll want to prepare the charcoal in this way when you are using it to paint rawhide or leather.

FLOATING THE CHARCOAL FOR COLLECTION

Chunks or ground-up charcoal does not mix well with water. Using water to make charcoal pigment or paint isn't very effective; however, using water to float your charcoal, so you can collect it for later use, is very effective. Picking through the campfire pit for charcoal is a dirty, dusty job, but if you throw a few shovels of ash into a bucket of water, the chunks of charcoal rise to the surface ash free and ready to use.

NOTE

Drawing on rocks with charcoal does not have the same permanent blackening effect that we find on fire pit rock rings. Without the heat of the fire to set the burn into the pores of the rock, and without the continual use of the same rock ring fire pit, charcoal drawing has no longevity. You could make a waterproof coating from plants to apply over your charcoal drawings, and they could last outside for several seasons. (See Make Your Own Paints with Earth Minerals, p. 145.) If you are going to have some fun doing this and you plan to camp at a public campground, bring along a little scrub brush and use water to erase your drawings before you go. Graffiti is a longstanding ancestral tradition, but its popularity has waxed and waned for millennia. Since it seems to currently be in the waning stage, washing yours away would be the thoughtful thing to do!

MAKE A MATCHLESS CAMPFIRE

Everything you learned about fire in the previous chapter applies here, and the only difference is that the bundle of flaming tinder replaces the match. Regardless of how you get the initial combustion or flame, you have to gather all your kindling and use your kindling-placement techniques to build your campfire successfully.

♠♠♠
MAKE A MATCHLESS CAMPFIRE USING A HAND DRILL

You have mastered campfire starting (and putting out) techniques and the one-match fire. Why not try making your fire by rubbing two sticks together? Seriously! This is a good time to learn this fire-making technique, which is called friction fire making. You now have enough know-how and experience from practicing fire starting that when you do get an ember from rubbing the two sticks, it will transmute into a flame, and you know how to be responsible with that flame.

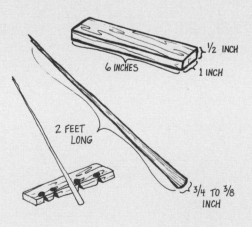

½ INCH

6 INCHES

1 INCH

2 FEET LONG

¾ TO ⅜ INCH

If you're just sitting around practicing the combustion part, like you did with your box of matches, then making embers all by themselves or blowing embers into flames once placed in a bundle of tinder is certainly a great time. However, if a campfire is what you're after, and especially if you really need one in a survival situation, there's no sense in going to all the effort of making a friction-fire ember unless you are prepared to transform it into a campfire.

THE TINDER BUNDLE

To make a campfire without matches, a lighter, or any other gadget or substance, gather your kindling first. Then you'll prepare a wicked good bundle of tinder. You need to have your tinder prepared and your little bundle all made up before you make the embers. You are going to mimic the shape of a bird's nest when you make this tinder bundle.

GATHER AND PREPARE THE MATERIALS

Find soft, very dry inner or outer bark that you can rough up into a

fuzzy, dusty mass. Over a flat rock, or some surface that allows you to save all the falling bark dust, scrub the bark together like you're washing out a pair of socks, until it is soft and pliable. Often, bark that seems very hard at first will soften as you work it. Place your back to the wind so the dust doesn't blow away as it falls.

MAKE A CONFINING RING

Once the bark is soft, stringy, and fuzzed up, take a length of it and wrap it into a little ring, twisting the ends over each other so they don't pull apart. Make the ring about the size of the circle you make with your thumbs and pointer fingers joined at the tips. If the lengths of bark aren't very long and are hard to twist into a ring, you can use something else, like long pieces of grass twisted together. This will even work with moist, green grass or plant material ➡

since this ring is just holding the rest of the nest together.

FORM THE NEST

Take the rest of the fuzzy material and stuff it into the ring in the shape of a nest. You have fuzzed up the bark to increase its surface area and make the tiniest little bits of dry tinder that will catch fire easily. If you stuff it all into the ring very hard and smash it down flat, you lose that increased surface area and you make it harder for oxygen to join the heat of the ember and combust. Stuff it in, but use a light touch. Make a small depression in the center, just like a nest. This is where you will put the leftover bark dust you didn't let blow away.

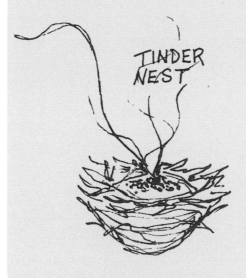

TINDER NEST

GATHER THE DUST

I have a specific way of picking up my bark dust and placing it in the tinder nest. In the same way that we would not hold a match to a large log and expect the log to catch fire, we do not place a tiny pile of glowing dust (our ember) into large, jagged, fuzzed up pieces of bark and expect the heat of the ember to transfer right away. The trick is to try to match the material in size, working up gradually, just like we did with our piles of kindling. We put the finest bark dust we create in the very top of the nest, which is where we will place the ember.

GO FOR THE GOLD

Using your fingertips, sweep all that fallen bark powder into a pile. As you sweep it together, the finest particles will sift to the bottom of the pile. Grab a big pinch of dust off the top of the pile with your fingertips, turn the pinch upwards, and place it into the center of the tinder nest. You will notice that the grains of bark powder you placed downward into the indentation of the nest are larger than the ones you've just settled into the top. It is a little tricky to pick up the pinch of

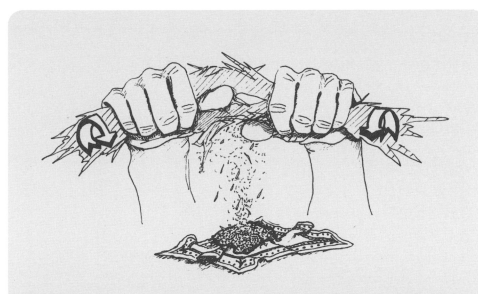

bark, flip it around, and place it into the nest without losing any, but it's worth the effort.

Sweep the pile back together with your fingertips before picking up the second pinch. Again, flip it upwards. See how fine the grains of bark powder are now? Sweep up whatever is left and place it at the very top. I call this last bark powder the "gold dust." Gold dust grains are very similar in size to the grains of your embers.

OPTIONS

If you can't find bark, you can use dried plant matter, grasses, or leaves, crushing them up into a powdery mass. If you have a very small amount of bark, use it to make the ring to hold these dried materials, or use the green grass. Instead of a ring, you could use a curved piece of hard bark to hold the dry matter. While you're playing around in the woods and practicing making your tinder bundles, be creative and try to make any kind of crazy tinder bundle you can think of. If you find yourself in a survival situation someday, your creativity and practice could really pay off.

Your piles of kindling are ready and waiting, and your wicked-good tinder bundle with its final layer of gold dust is set in a safe place nearby where you won't knock it over or step on it when you prepare your friction fire. Now you need to collect the two pieces of wood you will rub together to create an ember.

▲▲ MAKE A FRICTION DRILL

To create your fire-making set, you'll want your Old Hickory or a good stone knife. You are learning to make a Hand Drill Fire Set.

MAKE THE DRILL

For the first piece of wood, you want a long, cylindrical stalk that you can roll between the palms of your hands, applying pressure downward, so the lower tip of that stalk drills into your hearth board. You are looking for the straightest possible drill you can find. You don't want it to wobble as you drill down because it will be too hard to keep the drill pressing into the hearth board below. Straight drills don't wobble.

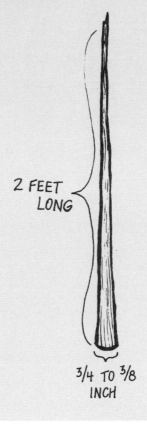

2 FEET LONG

3/4 TO 3/8 INCH

KNOWLEDGE

There are many kinds of plants that grow ready-made to become drills in fire sets. **Mullein**, **yucca**, **elderberry**, **horseweed**, **seep willow**, **goldenrod**, **cattail** and many other plants make good fire drills.

If you break or snap these stalks off at the bottom, they won't work for drilling. Splits and cracks will run up through the stalk, especially if the centers are pithy. Use your steel or stone knife to make small angled cuts all around the base of the stalk, going in slightly deeper each time you go round and round until you come to the center.

YUCCA

▲▲▲
MAKE THE HEARTH BOARD

The next piece of your set is called the hearth board or the baseboard. (This is the lingo used by experienced friction fire makers.) The drill will spin in the hearth board.

Knock off a ½-inch slab of wood from a larger branch or log, or split a smaller branch in half to make the hearth board for your fire set. You can set your steel knife at the edge of a larger piece of wood or center it in the middle of a smaller branch, and then knock the top end of the blade with a rock to send it straight down through the wood. This will make a flat, fairly smooth surface on at least one side of this piece of your set. If you split a branch instead of making a slab, it still needs to be ½-inch thick and a little more than two drill-widths wide after you have flattened one of the curved sides.

With the flat inner half of the branch facing up and vertically away from you, put your sharp edge on either side of the flat surface, at a perpendicular line to the flat surface, and split that down. Now you have a flat inner surface (the top) of your hearth board, for spinning the drill on, and a flat side, or edge. The flat edge is for carving a notch into the drill area that will hold the wood dust as the drill spins. This wood dust will drop into the notch and allow the ember to form.

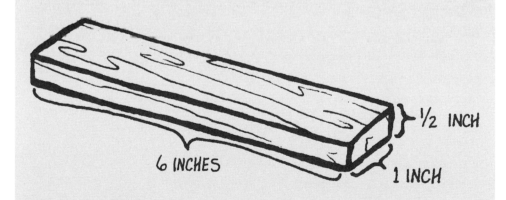

6 INCHES

½ INCH

1 INCH

KNOWLEDGE

You do not have to use the same kind of wood for both pieces of the fire set. Some woods work well when you use them for both the drill and the hearth board. Some work better combined with something else. Some good hearth board woods are **cottonwood**, **basswood**, **agave**, **yucca**, **cedar**, and **white pine**. Many any other varieties work well with the hand-drill method. Try the mullein on cottonwood, the horseweed on basswood, or the goldenrod on white pine. Experiment. You'll find many things that work.

IDEA

You can play a game with your friends of finding the greatest variety of materials in your area that make fire. Set up a big poster board, like a science fair poster board, and have everyone attach samples of the wood they used to make fire. It's a terrific way to get to know your outdoor home. If nothing more, it's a fun way to pass a few hours playing in the woods before heading back home for dinner. At some point though, it could make the difference to whether or not you make it home at all. Why not have a big bag of tricks?

♠♠ FINE-TUNE THE DRILL

Now that you've collected the two different pieces for your fire set, they need a little extra craftsmanship to fine-tune them for fire making. As for the drill, you want to take the blunt edge of your stone knife, set it perpendicular to the drill, and scrape the knife up and down with one hand as you spin the drill in your other hand. If it's a stalk that is too bumpy to spin while you scrape, like mullein or yucca, just support the drill on a flat surface and scrape one part of the drill at a time. You are not trying to remove a layer of material; rather, you are removing the rugosities, or roughness, so that when you rotate the drill between your palms, applying downward pressure, you won't beat up your hands. If the drill is gently smoothed, your hands won't get bruises and blisters that would prevent you from being able to spin the stalk.

REMOVE THE PITH

Many of the plants that make good drills have a pithy inner core. When you're drilling down to make an ember, the outer woody part of the stalk is the part wearing away to create the dust. The pith compresses with the pressure and hardens with the heat. Instead of wearing away into dust, it creates a little rounded tip in the center of the drill. This tip of hardened pith is too soft to penetrate the wood of the hearth board. Still, it is just hardened enough to hold the outer edges of the drill up and away from the hearth board, preventing the contact of the two woods while drilling, which prevents the dust being created for an ember. To get rid of the pith before you start your fire, take the pointy edge of your stone knife and rotate it lightly inside the bottom end of the stalk, removing some of the pith.

▲▲▲
FINE-TUNE OR SHAPE THE HEARTH BOARD

When you began your hearth board, you split off a ½-inch-thick slab from a large log or branch, or split a branch in half. Make sure you have about a ½ inch of depth to your hearth board, going down from the top flat surface, because you need to have some wood to wear away to create the dust that will form the ember. You don't want the board much thicker than this, or the dust drops down too far into the notch you will make, cooling off enough as it falls to prevent combustion.

Carve or adjust the bottom of the board so that when you set it flat on the ground, or a bench, or wherever you're going to make the fire, it sits steady and doesn't rock or tip. It does not have to be a perfect rectangular prism. You just need your flat upper surface, where the drill spins, to face upwards, and your flat side, where you carve the notch, to be pretty much perpendicular to the ground.

➡

KNOWLEDGE

You need enough accumulation of dust (caused by rubbing the two sticks together) and enough heat (caused by the pressure you exert and the speed with which you drill) to allow the little pile of dust to combust and become a glowing ember. If the pressure you exert when spinning the drill is creating heat too far away from the accumulation of dust, the temperature won't rise enough for combustion to happen.

DETERMINE PLACEMENT OF THE DRILL HOLE

You are going to spin the drill in the top flat surface of the hearth board, or "burn in" the drill hole. You need to choose this placement carefully.

QUESTION

Why? When you are done, the circumference (outer ring) of the burned-in hole closest to the flat side of your hearth board should be about ⅛ inch away from that flat edge. This will give you the right amount of wood to work with to form a notch. You carve a

GOUGE AN INDENTATION SO ITS EDGE IS ⅛ INCH FROM EDGE OF BASE-BOARD

little triangle notch out of the edge of the board into the center of the circle. The sides of the triangle-shaped notch are what contain the dust, keeping it in a pile. That's where your ember forms.

Make a little divot in the hearth board for the drill to sit. To place the divot, look at the base of the drill and get an estimate of its diameter. Now set the drill on the top flat surface of the hearth board so that the drill's outer edge is ⅛ inch from the flat-side edge of the board. Maybe use a pencil to draw a circle of the drill on the board top or use a sharp edge to mark the circle. Set the drill aside.

At the center of that circle, place the pointed tip of your stone knife, press it down, and rotate it back and forth to make a shallow conical indentation in the wood. You are making this divot so that you can set the tip of the drill into it and start spinning the drill until it seats slightly down into the hearth board. If you don't make the divot first, the drill will dance around on the top, not seating in anywhere, and spin right off the board. This is an exercise in frustration. It only takes a moment to make the divot with a sharp stone point.

BURN IN THE DRILL HOLE

Place your palms together and press them against each other at the top of the drill. Now roll the drill back and forth between your palms, pushing downward as you rotate. Control the drill so that it stays vertically straight. This is the exact spinning technique, or drilling, that you will use to make your ember. You are doing it now so that the drill base can burn into the hearth slightly, making a nice dark circle that allows you to know exactly where to carve your notch. Friction fire makers call this process "burning in the drill hole."

NOTE

As soon as you can see a nice defined circle and the drill seats in well, stop. You don't want to wear away a lot of the wood while you burn in the hole. Save the thickness of the board so that there is plenty of wood for making dust to create the ember. The drill can drill through the board pretty fast once you get the knack of it!

CARVE THE NOTCH

Hold your hearth board so that you are looking directly at the flat-side edge. This is the thinnest edge. Make sure the wider, top, flat side of the board is upward. Carve a notch into the side of the board that goes almost to the center of the burned-in hole. The shape of the notch is an isosceles triangle with the top point at the center of the burned-in hole. The base of the triangle is along the flat-side edge. This base should be about $3/8$ inch long. Place your steel blade at the outer edge of one side of

➡

the triangle, cutting in towards the center area, first one way and then the other, removing little wedges of wood as you go. Remember, the notch is getting thinner and thinner as you work your way up to the top point in the center of the burned-in hole. I like to outline the notch before I start carving, placing my blade along the outline and carving away everything in between.

TRY USING A STONE BLADE

If you are using a stone blade that has a triangular shape already, sometimes you can simply saw back and forth with the stone blade. If the stone blade is sturdy enough and slightly serrated, you can work your way to the point in the middle of the burned-in hole having made a perfect triangular notch shape.

FLARE THE TRIANGLE WALLS

This is not a geometry test, so it doesn't have to be perfect. You have the point of the triangle near the center of the hole and the base of the triangle along the flat-side edge of the hearth board. The two side edges of the triangle cut down through the depth of the hearth board, and this creates a triangle-shaped notch on the bottom of the board too. These edges or walls, going through the thickness of the hearth board, should flare out as they descend to the bottom of the board. This little flare allows the dust to drop freely through the notch.

GET THE NOTCH WIDTH JUST RIGHT

As you rotate the drill in the hearth board, the two woods wear away at each other and create dust. You want the dust to accumulate in a pile, so it's not much help if it catches up along the edges of the notch. The dust won't drop freely if the notch is too skinny either, and it may not get enough oxygen. Play around with it until you get it just right. You'll know what "just right" is because you'll have an ember!

If you carve out too wide of a triangular space, you will have taken away a good wedge of the burned-in hole area. The drill is spinning in that area and creating dust, so you don't want to lose too much of that wood. Also, a wide notch makes it harder to contain the heat, and you have to drill longer to collect enough dust in the notch space.

TRIANGULAR SHAPED
NOTCH FROM ABOVE

TRIANGLE APEX
AT CENTER

THE DRILL HOLE IS
1/8 INCH AWAY FROM BASEBOARD
EDGE

3/8 INCH WIDE AT
BASE OF TRIANGLE

1/4 INCH WIDE AT EDGE
OF DRILL HOLE

TRIANGULAR SHAPED
NOTCH FROM THE SIDE

1/16 INCH LIP
IN DRILL HOLE

1/2 INCH FLARE AT
BOTTOM OF BASE WOOD

MAKE THE HAND-DRILL FIRE

MAKE A LANDING PAD FOR YOUR DUST

Your set is made and fine-tuned. Your notch is carved just right. Now, place a little sliver of wood under the notch to catch the dust that drops there. When the ember forms, you can lift that little sliver of wood, keeping the ember intact, and gently tip the ember off the sliver into your tinder bundle.

STEADY THE HEARTH BOARD

Now secure your hearth board in place by driving a few wooden pegs into the ground at a sharp angle that pins down the board edges or by setting your foot securely on one end. You can also take another flat slab of wood and place it perpendicular to the hearth board. Place your knee

on one end of the slab, and let your body weight press the slab into the hearth board, holding it in place. If you are making a fire as part of a team, one person can hold the hearth board steady while the other person drills. When you switch tasks, make sure to hold the hearth board very steady so that it doesn't wiggle and knock the pile of dust where an ember may be forming.

SPIN THE DRILL

Follow the drilling directions given for burning in the hole on the hearth board. Speed helps increase heat. Each time you stop going one way and have to come back the other way, the drill isn't moving, so use the full length of your flattened palms and fingers as you rotate the drill to help keep up the speed. As you rotate the drill back and forth, concentrate on applying pressure down the length of the drill. This not only helps the drill stay seated in the hole but also assists in the formation of wood dust, as the two woods grind together with each rotation. The pressure also assists in creating heat.

CONSIDER

This fabulous little feat of maintaining rotational speed and downward pressure at the same time is a little bit tricky at first. Most of us don't play Beethoven's Fifth the first time we sit down at the piano. Another tricky part when you're starting is keeping the stalk planted firmly in the hole of the hearth board. If you do not keep the drill straight up and down as you rotate downward, the back and forth motion tends to pop the bottom tip of the drill out of the hole. Every time this happens, you lose a lot of heat. This delays combustion.

TECHNIQUE

When you rotate the drill with your flattened hands, you start at the top of the drill stalk and end up near the bottom. I call this "making one pass down the drill." When you lift your hands to make the second pass, leave one hand at the base, keeping the bottom tip of the drill secure in the hole of the hearth board, while you lift the other hand to the top. When you have the top hand pressing the stalk down securely, bring the lower hand up. If you try to lift both hands at once, you'll pop the bottom tip out of the hole. There goes your heat!

Every single time you try a pass down the drill, you are getting better. Every practice run brings you closer to creating fire. There is no elixir in this world that offers the jubilance of creating fire. Keep practicing!

TEAM FIRE MAKING

My favorite way to learn friction fire making is to work together as a team. One person makes a pass down the drill and then holds the bottom tip steady until the second person has their hands ready to go at the top of the drill. The trick is to try to keep the drill in constant motion. Sometimes, continual motion and speed of the drill allows an ember to form even if you haven't learned to apply good downward pressure yet. Having several team members at the ready helps the drill stay in motion and allows each person to really go for speed on their passes, knowing they'll have a rest in between passes.

You're developing a whole new pattern of muscle movement. Team fire building allows you to practice more, and for longer, than trying it all on your own. Who's to say you need to make a fire all on your own anyway? Making a fire by rubbing two sticks is a grand accomplishment, no matter how many people are on the team.

LOOK AND LISTEN

As you continue to rotate the drill with enough speed and pressure, you will hear a slight grating sound as the two woods grip into each other, and the drill base will start to smoke. The forming dust will start to darken, turning from light brown to dark black. At first the smoke will appear light gray and wispy, but as the heat increases, the smoke will thicken and turn creamy and yellowish. The dust will often appear to inch forward and buckle out from the edge of the notch, almost like an inchworm. Your fire set is giving you visual and audio clues to the development of the ember. At this point, the accumulation of dust, under the influence of the generated heat, coalesces, forming a small burning ember. Combustion! The formation of every ember is awe inspiring to me, no matter how many times I watch it happen.

You have an ember! Your tinder bundle is waiting. Set your fire drill down somewhere safe, where it won't get stepped on or mistaken for a stick to burn and thrown onto the fire!

COLLECT THE EMBER FROM THE NOTCH

Holding the hearth board steady with one hand, gently rap your knuckle on the top of the hearth board to loosen the ember from the notch. Lift the hearth board carefully, raising the notch edge first, and bring that edge back toward you, almost as if you were peeling it up and away, leaving the ember intact.

PLACE THE EMBER IN THE TINDER BUNDLE

The ember is usually sitting on the little sliver of wood you placed below the notch. Sometimes it worms its way forward and onto the ground, or it grows so big that it spills off the sides of the wood sliver. If this happens, carefully slide your knife blade (or another sliver of wood) under the ember, and lift it into the center of your tinder bundle, right into the waiting gold dust.

Rejoice! Now is the time to take a deep full breath, steady yourself, and take a few seconds for your smile to spread from ear to ear! You

have made an ember by rubbing two sticks, and you have safely transferred it into your waiting nest of tinder. Each step of this process is a skill all its own. Each step accomplished is a great success. Stay focused and confident and you will soon blow your ember into a flame.

GROW YOUR EMBER

You need to find the right finger pressure to contain the ember in the bundle, gently folding in the sides of the tinder nest to enclose the ember, but still allowing it enough air. Then very gently and almost imperceptibly, begin to blow a steady stream of air across the ember, allowing it to grow and expand into the waiting bark dust surrounding it. Remember, heat rises. Gently lift the bundle and tilt the bottom slightly upward, making sure the ember is secured, and blow air up into the bundle, allowing the heat to rise and spread throughout the nest.

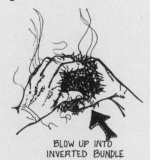

BLOW UP INTO
INVERTED BUNDLE

KNOWLEDGE

There are several reasons why a tinder bundle does not burst into flame. One common reason is that once you place the ember into the center of the tinder bundle, it is very easy to pinch the tinder bundle up too tightly around the ember and smother it. Remember, fire needs oxygen.

Another common reason is that you begin to blow on the little ember with too much force. This blows the ember apart, scattering it into little bits of spark that are too small and not hot enough to catch the surrounding bark dust on fire.

TIP

Keep your back to the breeze so that the smoke won't blow into your face. When you're crying and choking, it's hard to finesse a tinder bundle into flame. If you are tired, starting to hyperventilate, or having trouble blowing the ember, hold the tinder bundle opening toward the breeze and let the air work for you. You can also swing the tinder bundle in a repeated pattern of the infinity symbol (Geez! Everything is a math lesson, no?), using the air movement instead of your breath to blow the ember into flame. As you swing your arm in the controlled and repeated loops, have the top end of the tinder nest, where you deposited the ember, facing into the air. This works well, but do it calmly.

You will see the wispy gray smoke begin to turn creamy, yellow, and thick just before combustion. Move closer to the fire pit and your kindling pile when you see the smoke making this transition. When the tinder bundle bursts into flames, shout for joy and gratitude, and then place it upside down in the fire pit (perhaps on a few sticks set there to allow air to still come into the bottom of the bundle), letting the flames rise up through the nest and catch more of the bark on fire. Quickly and deftly place your kindling sticks above and around the burning nest. If the flames begin to sputter, lean down very low and gently blow towards the bottom of the nest, helping the flames rise up into the tinder.

SURVIVAL SHELTERS

Knowing how to make a shelter that is safe and maintainable, appropriate for the weather conditions, and keeps out the elements, with the least possible energy output, is good knowledge.

CONSIDER

If you are low on energy, finding shelter that will meet all your practical needs, instead of creating one, is a good idea. It isn't always possible out in the wild, but it is probable. A very important consideration when looking for shelter that is already available is whether or not it is already occupied. Although setting up house in a lion or a bear cave makes a much better story, the truth is that you usually find yourself trying to move in with much smaller critters, like a variety of rodents, snakes, or spiders. Well, now that I think about it, the stories I have about these kinds of mishaps are pretty big stories. Anyway, you get the point.

SHOCKING KNOWLEDGE

If you are seeking temporary shelter from a rainstorm, it is important to understand how lightning works. Even if you don't see any evidence of lightning, electrical currents are on the move during storms. Although a lightning strike seems to be only coming down from the clouds, a shocking charge, which is the part that is so dangerous to you, is running straight up out of the ground. When storms form in the sky and the friction and chaos above begins to create an electric charge, the ground offers contact, or release, for that charge. As the current shoots upward from the ground, the charge is formed in the clouds and shoots downward to connect to that ground charge. If you happen to be standing in that area, you become the most convenient conduit, or pathway, for the electricity. Bad news!

Most people have heard that you don't want to stand in an area with a very tall tree or a large metal flagpole or be out on the golf course with your number six iron raised. Just like the spark plug in a car, the charge wants to jump the easiest path to the ground. If you find shelter under overhanging rock during a highly charged storm, your body will act just like the spark plug. Although the overhang seems like wonderful shelter, it could be a poor and perhaps lethal choice.

Getting metal things off your body during an electrical storm should be a priority. Ball caps with little metal buttons on the top, rucksacks with metal components, hiking poles, and even tent poles carried inside your pack should be set down and moved away from. An even higher priority is to get out of any standing water. Most of us are familiar with being asked to exit the outdoor swimming pool when a lightning storm passes overhead. Water and metal are very good lightning attractors because they create an easy pathway for the current to travel through. Even standing in a small puddle on the trail makes you a better pathway for electricity.

THE LIGHTNING POSITION

If you find yourself in an area where there is simply nowhere to go for shelter from lightning, you can squat down over your rubber-soled shoes and cross your forearms over your chest with your hands gripping their opposite shoulders. I have used this lightning position many times. The idea is that electricity wants to move through the easiest path, so if you place your hands on the ground to steady yourself, the charge will move right up one arm, through your heart, and out the other arm—the quickest path to ground. This is why you keep your arms crossed with your hands upon your shoulders. If the squatting position gets uncomfortable, sitting back on your bottom creates another direct pathway for current, unless perhaps you are wearing rubber pants! Rubber is not a good conductor of electricity, and this is why being directly over the soles of your shoes can help keep you from becoming nature's spark plug.

LIGHTNING AND VEHICLES

It is not uncommon for people to have stories about their vehicles being struck by lightning. The rubber tires are insulating you from the wet, current-charged ground, even though you are encased in a metal box. Get any metal in the vehicle away from you, and don't touch any metal parts of the framework while the lightning is active. You can use the same lightning position for your arms and hands. When lightning strikes your vehicle, it can burn up your entire electric system while leaving you completely unharmed. Well, at least physically.

ELIMINATE FEAR

It's important to talk about how to be safe in stormy conditions outdoors because severe weather conditions prevent many people from taking the opportunity to spend more time outside. With knowledge and skill development, you can eliminate fear. So often the woods are perceived as a dangerous place. If you think about a lot of our fairy tales, myths, and legends, and even many stories in the Bible, the wilderness is often portrayed as an undesirable place. Great fires and floods take lives; earthquakes swallow people. The animals that live in our outdoor home are often portrayed in these stories as dangerous or tricky, leading the protagonist to disaster. It's easy to understand why many of us experience anxiety when thinking about the wilderness or wild animals. Often these concerns are unconscious, subtly spoon-fed into our psyche over many years.

CONSIDER

How interesting then that so much research is being done on the physiological and psychological benefits of being in nature. For many years, people who enjoy the outdoors have been able to wax eloquent on the wonderful feeling of being open, free, and at home in nature (think Thoreau, John Muir, the biblical Songs of Solomon, Aldo Leopold . . .). What's riveting about the current nature-immersion research is the quantifiable data being collected shows reductions in blood pressure and stress-hormone levels when people choose to be in a natural environments. What a perfect time to be thinking about how to play in the woods!

TAKE ACTION

A comfortable shelter can make you feel much more at home in the woods. Unlike many animals, people do not have thick hides or heavy fur, and curling up to wait out the weather doesn't work very well for us. We've already talked about shelters in wild places for fun, play, and to create a homey, personal spot (see Make Shelters and Forts for Fun, p. 53). However, when we create a shelter for survival, we have some practical considerations to take into account that don't really apply when we are just kickin' about having a good time. Staying dry and warm is the best thing we can do for ourselves if we are out in the woods without a tent, tarp, or layers of appropriate outdoor clothing.

A good shelter keeps us dry and warm. You might be lost, you could have just stayed out too long and not be able to make your way back home in the dark, or you could be immobilized by a temporary weather situation. Shelter-building principles are the same for whatever conditions you find yourself in. Your building resources are all around you. Who knows what those are going to be? Your job is to be resourceful and creative with what you have. As Teddy Roosevelt said, "Do what you can, with what you have, where you are." With a little creativity and a willingness to get the job done, there is almost nothing you can't do.

CITY OR WOODS

Across the urban areas of the world, homeless people show resourcefulness and persistence in creating shelters for their survival. Insulation for warmth is made with crumpled newspapers, cloth layers, or used clothes, and moisture is deflected by bits of metal, plastic, or coated cardboard. In more natural environments, insulation can be layers of dried plant material, grasses, piles of fluffed-up seed heads like milkweed or cattail, or layers of pine needles or dried leaves.

IMPORTANT

As you collect these materials, make sure they aren't already the home of ants, scorpions, snakes, or other things that you don't want to cuddle with!

STAY DRY

A moisture barrier can be a roof made of large slabs of bark, a selection of logs, or sticks with layers of plant and leaf material or pine needles on top; or it could simply be the low-hanging, sheltering boughs of a large tree or shrub. In my area, you can almost always find a dry spot to curl up under a spruce tree, even in a heavy rain. Rock overhangs can also provide shelter from moisture, but keep in mind what we mentioned about lightning. Additionally, if it's raining and the overhang is along the banks of a waterway, flash flooding is a serious consideration.

IMPORTANT

If you can get a fire started, a rock overhang can radiate with warmth through the night. Position the fire just outside the lip of the overhang, and the heat will reflect off the back walls and ceiling. If you get the fire too far into the overhang or get it too hot, the heat can make large slabs of rock fall off the underside of the overhang. Bad news!

INSULATION

Layer thick piles of pine needles or dried plant material to insulate you from the ground. If you're short on material, concentrate on insulating yourself from your head to the top of your legs. The main trunk of your body is generating the most heat. The ground will absorb any heat your body creates, especially if it is rocky, sandy mineral soil or has a lot of moisture. Making a sufficient insulation layer below you is often just as important as having enough material above you. If there is no wind and the air is not very cold, insulation below you might be more important.

MAKE A SHELTER

GET OUT OF THE WIND

You will want to create a wind block for your shelter to keep the air from blowing over you and taking away your body heat by **convection**. Placing your shelter in the lee (the side opposite from where the wind is blowing) of trees, shrubs, boulders, or hillsides is a good idea. Often, you can find a big tree trunk lying on the ground. Not only can you use this to block the wind and to prop other sticks and logs to create a roof, but also, if the trunk has been lying there for a while, the bark will have loosened and can easily be lifted away from the trunk to use for your shelter.

BUILD A BARK SURVIVAL SHELTER

Take a sharp stone edge and cut the bark so that you can lift a whole half circle of bark covering off the trunk. Try to get one piece as long as your body, but if you can't, then line up a bunch of smaller pieces. Lay the bark down, curved edges up, on the lee side of the trunk, and fill it with soft, dry insulation materials. It will look like a nature cradle. Take another slab of curved bark for a covering. Lay it down right next to the other piece, and fill it up with good insulation.

When you are ready to snuggle in and sleep warm and dry, get yourself into the first cradle, and then reach over and lift the second cradle up and over, putting it on top of you. It helps if you keep your eyes squeezed shut and have a hood on your sweatshirt to tie tight under your chin, but you are, after all, in a survival situation, and you have just created a wonderful, workable shelter. So what are a few pine needles down the neck?

BURROW FOR SHELTER

Simply burrowing into a big pile of leaves or pine needles is another great way to stay warm and relatively dry. Even if the leaves and needles are slightly damp or wet, you will be able to maintain your heat if you can burrow right into the center. If you have the time and energy to strip some flexible bark fiber from some of the plants we've talked about (see Make String and Rope from Plant Fibers, p. 15), it's a good idea to tie the wrists of your shirt and ankles of your pants closed so that little scratchy bits don't go up your sleeves and pant legs. You can use this tying method and stuff dry grasses and

plant materials into all the areas of your clothing. Pine needles aren't so great for this, but if that's all you've got, use them.

MAINTAIN BODY HEAT

Many people have survived long, cold nights in nylon hiking shorts and a cotton T-shirt. Activity generates heat. The cliché of doing jumping jacks to warm up or running around in circles really works. Even a T-shirt can keep you warm if you tuck your knees up inside it and pull your arms in from the holes. A lot of your body heat escapes through the top your head and around your neck area, so if you can keep this area covered, you can maintain a lot more heat. With the T-shirt pulled up around your head and neck, put your forehead on your knees and breathe out your warm breath into your lap.

TIP

Remember, cold air sinks; warm air rises. If you locate your shelter in the bottom of a gully or along a watercourse, the cooler night air will settle there. Often, waterways are wind corridors, as are ridge tops and exposed flat areas, and wind takes your warmth away.

KNOWLEDGE

In winter conditions, many of these principles still apply; however, if you are in very snowy country, a snow cave or a quinzee are good options. A snow cave is dug into a large drift or hillside of snow. A quinzee is built when you pile up a large mound of snow and then dig into the mound. My favorite book on snow caves is *Snow Caves for Fun and Survival* by Ernest Wilkinson. Over the last six decades, Ernie has been a treasured teacher and mentor to thousands interested in survival and outdoor living. He trained and lived with many of the animals seen on the *Wild Kingdom* TV shows.

YOUR NUMBER ONE SURVIVAL SKILL

Your best shelter is a positive attitude. You know so much. Think about all the options, put ideas together, and come up with solutions. Stay busy. We've been talking about lots of fun activities to do out in the woods. If you've done everything you can to shelter yourself and stay safe, do some of those fun activities to keep yourself occupied. In his amazing book about hiking the Pacific Crest Trail, *A Thru-Hiker's Heart,* "No Way" Ray Echols wrote, "There are supporters out there, looking for you . . . waiting for you." He wasn't talking about being lost out in the woods, but I think this is a lovely idea to keep in mind, no matter the situation. If you are lost, someone—or lots of someones—are looking for you. Be calm, trust, and stay positive.

CONSIDER

This book isn't really about survival. My intention is to inspire you to spend more time outside, in nature, playing in the woods. And now there is scientific evidence to show it's best for your radiant well-being! That ought to convince you! That said, I wouldn't tell you the most fun stores to shop in while in downtown Chicago without also telling you how to get there, how to stay safe while taking the elevated train or bus downtown, and how to handle certain city situations with which you might be unfamiliar. I want you to go have a great time, see all the shows, find the best restaurants, and come back happy and amazed. Even so, out in the woods!

SURVIVAL TIPS

We are talking about how to see and participate in all the best nature shows, enjoy the best wild food, and feel happy and amazed throughout the experience. Thus, talking about how to stay safe and handle unpredicted situations is perfectly appropriate. On that note, since we've already brought up survival in this discussion about shelters, this is the right place to mention a helpful "Carry-Along" list.

SURVIVAL RESEARCH

As we say at Earth Knack, it is possible to head out into the wilderness with nothing, absolutely nothing, and not only survive, but thrive. John and Geri McPherson authored a book series called Naked into the Wilderness. They are my favorite books on the subjects of wilderness and primitive-living skills and survival. As the series title suggests, the books have all kinds of survival information. They would be useful for research if you plan to spend a lot of time out in wild areas, or even so you can be prepared in urban areas when modern systems are not available.

How to Play in the Woods is about creating a bridge for you and your friends and family to retreat from modern lifestyles and spend more time in nature. It is about role modeling nature immersion for our young ones. On that note, taking along a backup pack of survival equipment can add to the security you feel, encouraging you to step off the sidewalk more often, climb a few more trees, venture farther into the woods, have fun being "at home" in nature, and feel capable, confident, and happy doing so. After you pack your bag, write a note to leave at home that includes the general area where you are heading and when you plan to return.

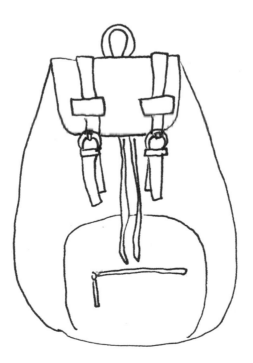

CARRY-ALONG LIST

- *water bottle full of water (stainless steel so that you can boil water when it gets empty)*
- *a snack*
- *Old Hickory sheath knife*
- *box of waterproof matches **and** a lighter*
- *petroleum jelly–coated cotton balls (to help the fire burn when you strike the match and light your kindling, especially in wet weather. Make them yourself and keep in a waterproof container.)*
- *raincoat and pants*
- *small plastic tarp with a 10-foot string tied to each corner and the two center grommets*

That's all folks! With these items alone, you can happily spend a lot of time in the woods, no matter what conditions you encounter. Plus, these can all fit into a very small daypack. We talked about weathering out a rainstorm and described spending the night out in just a pair of nylon shorts and a T-shirt; I think you can imagine what a luxury it would be to have a lightweight rain suit. It would be great for stuffing insulation inside of, be an excellent wind break, make sleeping in a bark-cradle shelter much more comfortable, and help you avoid getting wet in the first place.

HYPOTHERMIA

Many people have experienced the mind-and-body-crippling effects of hypothermia in damp, rainy weather that isn't really that cold. Hypothermia starts when your body temperature drops from its usual 98.6 degrees Fahrenheit and you start to shiver. If your temperature continues to drop, you can lose control of your basic motor functions, making things like striking a match or zipping up your coat almost impossible. Walking becomes difficult, and finally, you become mentally confused and unable to think about solutions.

A lightweight rain suit in your daypack is good insurance against hypothermia (plus, it's bugproof). It's kind of like having a wearable shelter. In a pinch, if you needed to collect water, you could tie the pant legs closed and haul a couple gallons to your shelter area! I just thought that up, so I bet you could think of three or four more uses right off the top of your head.

THINK SURVIVAL

Often when people look for outdoor clothing, natural camouflage colors are popular. There is this unspoken understanding that people who care about the environment try to blend in when they're out in nature. If you get a rain outfit or a tarp in a bright neon color, it will be much more useful to you in a survival situation. Your shelter and clothing become signaling devices. Now you think of some more survival tricks!

CONSIDER THE HUMBLE TARP

Let me tell you why I love tarps: They are windproof and waterproof. You can wrap them around you for a hooded rain poncho. You can roll up inside them for a sleeping bag. You can string them up high and flat, making a shady place in hot weather that the breeze can flow through. You can pitch them low and steeply angled in rain or snow and have a tight, protected shelter. You can haul water in them. You can make a solar still with a tarp. (This is when you set a tarp over a pit full of moist materials in the sunshine, creating condensation that provides you with drinkable water. Very cool!) If they are brightly colored, you can use them to signal, or you can cut strips and mark the trail. They make a lot of noise when you shake them and spread them out; this is a great way to chase away animals you haven't invited into your camp. They are very lightweight. You can carry them to the top of a 14,000-foot mountain and prop them up on the summit as a nice little windproof enclosure while you eat your lunch. Folded up in several layers, they make great insulated pads to sit or lie on. You can hold a tarp up in your canoe during a strong wind and use it as a sail. A tarp is easy and quick to set up, creating a windproof, waterproof home to protect you and your gear in just a few minutes.

QUESTION

Are you ready to become a tarp convert? To fulfill the requirements of truth in advertising, the one possible drawback is they aren't very bug proof unless you are completely wrapped up in them, which makes doing anything else quite impossible. However, you do have a rain suit, which is bugproof. If you're really concerned about bugs, you can find a simple mosquito head net that weighs almost nothing and compresses into the size of your fist. It's not on the list, but it could be, seeing as you could catch fish or crawdads in it, set it up like a snare, use it as a berry-picking basket, or fill it up with dry insulation material and stick your head or feet in the middle of it on a cold night.

GATHER WILD FOOD IN THE COUNTRYSIDE

Have you started collecting some of the foods described earlier and incorporating them into your regular meals? If so, perhaps you are already researching the authors I mentioned, who have written my favorite books on wild food and medicine. Their books will be a great resource as you increase your knowledge of wild plants.

QUESTION

Ready to look farther afield for more options? As you get farther from the edges of developed areas, you'll begin to find greater quantities of the wild foods we've already discussed and a greater variety of other wild foods.

KNOWLEDGE

Many colonies of wild plants with edible roots thrive in less-developed areas. Depending on where you live, **Indian potato** (southeast), **camas** (northwest), and **spring beauty** (Rocky Mountains) are a few wild plants that produce corms, or tubers, that can be prepared in the way you might prepare potatoes. **Wild onions** and the delectable **ramps** of the southeast are easy to recognize.

RESOURCE

Wild Roots is a book by Doug Elliott. It is a wonderful resource for the often overlooked wild foods that grow underground. **Cattail roots** are a nice starchy meal, and there are many books that give great preparation methods. During riparian restoration projects, cattail is often planted along the waterways because cattail roots are thought to enhance water quality by filtering out undesirable elements in the water.

IMPORTANT

Because of this filtering, it's important to collect your cattail roots from clean water sources. For that matter, think about where you are harvesting any wild foods. Many roadsides and open fields, as well as agricultural areas, have been treated to reduce weeds or pests and for many other reasons. Be thoughtful.

KNOWLEDGE

Spring is a great time to collect fresh, juicy roots and lower stalks of edible plants. The plants have not put their energy toward creating leaves or flowers yet, and their potency is concentrated in their newly developing roots and lower stalks. Many roots like **oyster root** or **Jerusalem artichoke** lose their crunchy, moist texture, becoming hard and woody, once they produce flowers. Some tubers are not developed until later in the season. Be patient when harvesting these plants; they will not taste good or store well if you pick them too soon.

In a stand of **amaranth**, **lamb's quarter**, or **nettle**, you can quickly gather several paper bags full of seed to store through the winter. Make sure the seed is fully ripened before you collected it. When it is ready to collect, it will have darkened completely, and begin to drop when you touch it.

AMARANTH   LAMB'S QUARTER   NETTLE

COLLECT WILD PLANT SEED FOR FOOD

The easiest way I know to collect the seed is to tip the seed head of the plant downward into an open paper bag. Squeeze the bag shut with both hands around the stalk of the plant, trapping the seed head upside down in the bag. Now shake the stalk like you are choking it, and all the seeds will fall into the bottom of the bag. Have another bag ready to dump the collected seeds into each time. Don't keep shaking the same bag over and over. If you do this, the bottom of the bag almost always splits open, or the sides rip.

IDEA

As long as you're collecting seeds, you might as well collect enough to plant all around areas closer to home. Cultivating wild plants in and around your homestead or neighborhood helps the spread of healthful wild, free food. Planting Jerusalem artichoke root or **rose hip** would be a wonderful addition to any area, but remember, a lot of the wild edible plants are seen as pernicious weeds. It's better to go out

ROSE HIP

searching for those than to bring them into neighborhoods where other people are constantly trying to eradicate them. These wild foods are about well-being; good community relations and lack of conflict are good foundations for all around well-being.

KNOWLEDGE

Many wild foods are not ready to collect until late fall or early winter. **Currant berries** are actually easier to pick once they have slightly withered and dried. They are good plump and fresh on the bush in mid-summer, but they get even sweeter after the first frost, which brings out their sugars. This is true with lots of seeded fruits, such as apples for example. I make jelly with currant berries, or dry them and store them in jars to eat through the winter. Rose hips are much tastier in early or mid-winter when they have withered and sweetened and their outer covering is like a little piece of fruit leather. As you get to know the wild foods in your area, you will become familiar with the best harvesting times.

CURRANT BERRIES

MAKE MEALS ON THE CAMPFIRE COALS

Cooking foods on the fire is a lot of fun and seems to make everything taste better. Here are some very easy things you can try to get started cooking on a bed of coals.

COOKING FISH ON THE COALS

If you fish, you're in for a treat when you roast your fish on the coals. Scrape a nice little pile of coals to the windward edge of the fire pit. Flatten down the coals, make an indentation in the center, and shape them to be big enough to hold your full fish. Set your clean and gutted fish, dorsal fin down, in the indentation.

When the flesh is no longer translucent and flakes off with a fork, it is ready to eat. You can lift it out and set it on a fire pit rock to cool for a moment. When the fish is cool enough to lift with your hand, peel out the skeleton and eat the meat right out of the skin—it's a ready-made dish.

KNOWLEDGE

It takes a little bit of time to learn the right kind of heat that you need from the coals to roast the fish slowly enough to keep it sizzling but quickly enough that it will remain moist. If you place it on very hot coals, it cooks very quickly, arching up immediately and lifting out of the indentation, and the skin oils dry up too fast and the meat turns dry. When you have the right heat, you usually don't have to move the fish around at all.

COOKING ASH CAKES ON THE COALS

A few scant cups flour, somewhere
between 2 and 3 cups
Several shakes salt, about 1/2
teaspoon
1 heaping teaspoon baking powder
Water to make dough

MAKE THE DOUGH

An ash cake is a circular patty of quick-rise bread. Mix together the flour, salt, and baking powder in a ziplock bag and shake the bag to mix well. Roll down the top edges of the bag and add the liquid, stirring it into the flour mix. (Using a ziplock bag instead of a bowl is a really good camping trick.) Slowly add enough water to form a dough ball you can handle without it sticking to your fingers. You do not want a sticky mess, but rather a ball of dough that you can move easily between your lightly floured hands. If you add too much water, add more flour.

PREPARE THE COALS

Spread out and flatten a large bed of coals on the windward edge of the fire pit. If the coals are too hot, the ash cakes will be burnt on the outside and raw on the inside. Let the coal bed cool down enough so that the ash cakes will brown well within 1–2 minutes on one side without burning. When you flip it over, it will take the second side a lot less time to brown.

COOK THE ASH CAKES

Lightly flour your fingertips, pinch off a small amount of the dough ball, and pat and stretch the dough into the shape of a miniature Frisbee. When you stretch the dough outward, don't tear it. Just prepare one ash cake at a time, and get it on the coals. While it's cooking, you can prepare the next one. When the ash cake is browned and cooked though, blow off the ash dust and flick off any small bits of clinging coal. It's fun and easy, and everyone can make their own. How many ash cakes you can make with this recipe is up to you. Make a lot of little ones or even try making one great big one. The thinner you pat them out the more you can make, and they will cook more quickly.

➡

RECIPE VARIATION

I like to add things to my ash cakes sometimes. I will put cinnamon and ginger or raisins into the dough to make something sweet. When they come off the coals, you can dip them in powdered sugar or put a little honey on them. If you add basil, chopped garlic, cracked pepper, and some grated cheese into the dough, you can pull them off the fire and dip them into a warm, yummy pizza sauce. Whatever you can think of, it's worth trying. It can be a fun, easy, active dinner for the whole crew.

BAKE POTATOES IN THE COALS

Baking potatoes or sweet potatoes can be buried down into the ash layer just below a coal bed. You can cook other things on the fire above them, or simply enjoy the fire until they are ready. It takes some practice to learn how to bury the potatoes just right, and to place them in a good part of the fire to cook well and evenly, but over time you will get better.

How long you cook the potatoes depends on what size they are and how much heat is in the coals. Poke them with a stick now and then to test them for softness. When they are done, set the potatoes on the fire pit rocks to cool. When you can handle them, all you have to do is brush off the ash; you can even eat the skin. Alternatively, you can rinse them off with water before eating the skin, but it's a good thing to eat the skin either way, because it has so many good vitamins and minerals.

ROAST CORN IN THE COALS

Lots of campers already know the roasting corn in the campfire trick. If you haven't done this before, you're in for a treat. While you're setting up camp, put the unshucked corn into a pot of water with all the stalk ends sticking up. Don't cut the stalk ends off.

Prepare your fire and build up a good bed of coals, all the while keeping the corn soaking in the pot. When you have a nice coal bed ready, place the soaked ears of corn, husk, stalk, and all, on the coals. If the coals are too hot, the corn will cook too quickly and not taste nearly as good. Using the uncut stalk ends, slightly rotate the ears of corn every so often. Peek into the husk now and then, checking for a light golden color to show they are done. The timing will depend on the freshness of the corn, its moisture content, and the heat of the coals. When the corn is ready, pull it out and let it cool down. Grabbing the stalk end as a handle, peel back the husks and the corn is ready to eat.

Fish, ash cakes, potatoes, and corn. That makes a whole meal, and you haven't dirtied a single dish! So what about dessert?

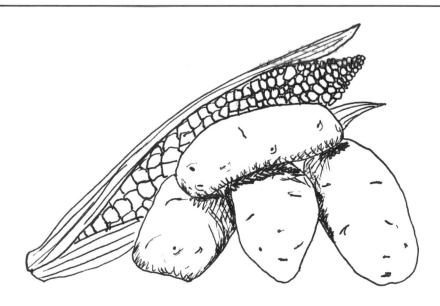

▲▲▲
BAKE A CAKE IN THE COALS

*Prepared cake mix that only
requires water (no eggs)*
*Large oranges (number will depend
on the size of the oranges, you
need to fill each peel halfway)*
*Water, as called for in the mix
instructions*

Here's a kick-in-the-pants recipe!
Before you go out into the woods,
make up your own chocolate cake
mix, mixing all the dry ingredients
together, or use a prepared mix
that only requires water, and put in
a ziplock bag.

PREPARE THE ORANGES AS BAKING PANS

Cut the top quarter off of each
orange at the stem end where the
fruit was attached to the tree. Take
a tablespoon and carefully scrape
the fruit out of the peels, keeping
the peels completely intact, and set
the fruit aside. Be sure to keep the
tops of the oranges, the caps, and
remove the fruit from them, too.

MIX THE CAKE BATTER

Now add the water to your cake
mix in the plastic bag. Keep the
bag upright and seal it. Use your
other hand to mix up the batter
from the outside of the bag. When
the batter is mixed well, cut off a
little corner of the bottom of the
bag. Squeeze batter out of the
hole in the bottom and fill each
orange-peel container halfway.

BAKE IN THE COALS

Put the little peel caps on the
oranges, and nestle these orange-
peel baking pans into a mildly hot
bed of coals. If you have the coals
too hot, they will burn right through
the orange peel. Baking time will
vary depending on the thickness of
the orange peels and the heat of
the coals. Usually 15–20 minutes
is enough for the small amount of
mix in each orange. To check the
cakes for doneness, skewer the
orange cap with a thin stick and lift
the cap to see if the cake is done
inside. It should spring back to your
touch. You can eat the oranges
while the chocolate cake is baking.
See how much fun this is? And
you still don't have any dirty dishes.
The amount of cakes you can make
with this recipe will depend on the
size of the oranges you use.

MAKE A FOIL MEAL

Another way to avoid dishes is to make foil meals. Use the heavy-duty aluminum foil and double layer it. You will make one packet for each serving. Prepare the ingredients below and use amounts of each ingredient in individual foil packets according to individual preference.

Finely chopped onion
Grated carrot
Diced potato
Oil
Spices
Ground meat

Toss the onion, carrot, and potato in a little bit of oil and all your favorite spices, coating the pieces well. Take a handful of ground meat or poultry, set it right in the middle of the top rectangle of foil, and cover it with the vegetable mix. (Make sure the two pieces of foil are large enough to wrap up the food and seal the edges. If you make the piece of foil too small, the juices will leak out, the food will burn easily, and it won't taste as good.) Don't forget to add a layer of lamb's quarter, watercress, or other wild greens you have collected. Chunks of fruit in the vegetable mix are also yummy.

Pull up the two cut ends of the foil, match the edges, and fold them down together at least three times, until they are tight over the food. Now turn the foil sheet a quarter turn, match the edges, and fold them at least three times inward; repeat with the remaining side. All the folded edges should come to the top of the foil package. Flip the first package over, edges down, and center it on the second piece of foil. Wrap that second piece in the same way.

COOK

Bury the entire package in a bed of mildly hot coals, and let it cook for about 30 minutes. When you pull the package out, the foil will be much more fragile after having been cooked. You might want to have some kind of wood plank or plate ready so that you can gently lift the package onto a supported platform. It's no fun to have all that yummy food dump into the coal and ash!

MAKE A BONE KNIFE OR AWL

Out in the woods, coming across deer leg bones and other kinds of bones is common. Bones make good hammers, instruments, decorations, and lots of other things.

MAKE A BONE KNIFE

Making a bone knife is as simple as finding a piece of bone and shaping it how you want. You can carve bone with a stone or steel knife, or you can grind it down on a more abrasive surface like a piece of sandstone or slate or a sidewalk. This is also an easy way to make spoons, fish hooks, and weaving shuttles. Here's a tip: if you split a deer leg bone in half, you get a flatter surface to work with, which makes it easier to grind out or carve the shape of what you want.

SPLIT A DEER LEG

To split a deer leg in half out in the woods, prop it up in the soil so that it is perpendicular to the ground. Take a sharp wedge of rock, one you find or make, or your metal knife, and set the blade in the center of the top of the bone. Place it so that as you hammer the sharp edge down into the bone, it will follow the grooves in either side of the leg bone where the tendons used to sit.

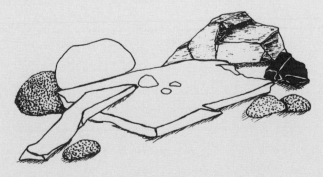

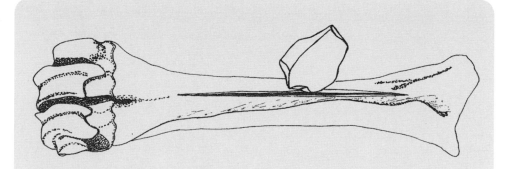

SCORING

These indentations running along the length of the bone are obvious. Before you try to split the bone, take the sharp edge of a sturdy rock and run it back and forth in these indentations, making a good groove, or score, on each side; it will split more easily and more evenly, following the score line.

MAKE A BONE AWL

A lot of times, if you don't score the bone first, it won't split cleanly all the way down to the bottom; rather, the blade will run over and out of the bone partway down. This actually gives you a pretty good shape for making a bone awl. An awl is a pointed tool that pokes holes in things for sewing, but it also pries things open or up. You will want a bone awl for making baskets, which we will talk about in Make a Bark Basket, p. 213, and Make a Rope Coil Basket, p. 219.

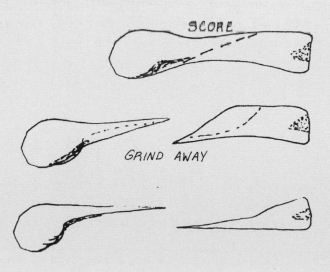

SCORE

GRIND AWAY

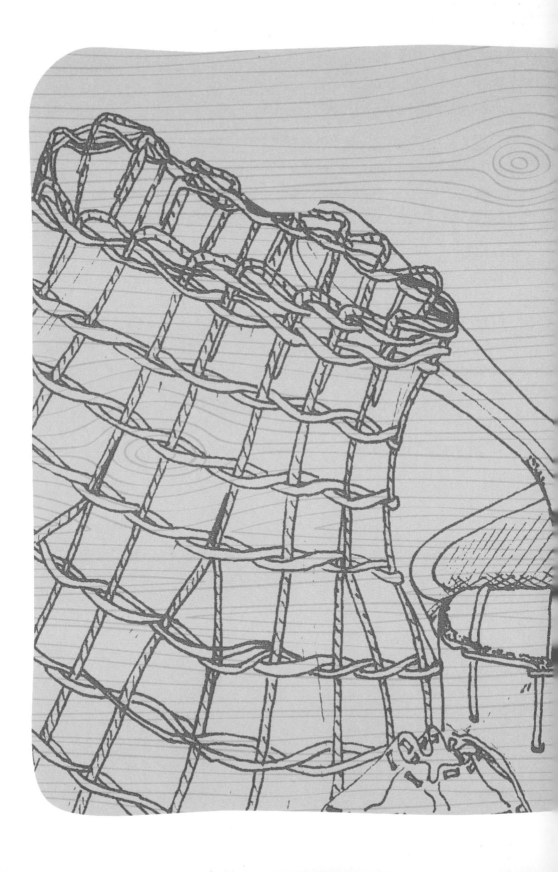

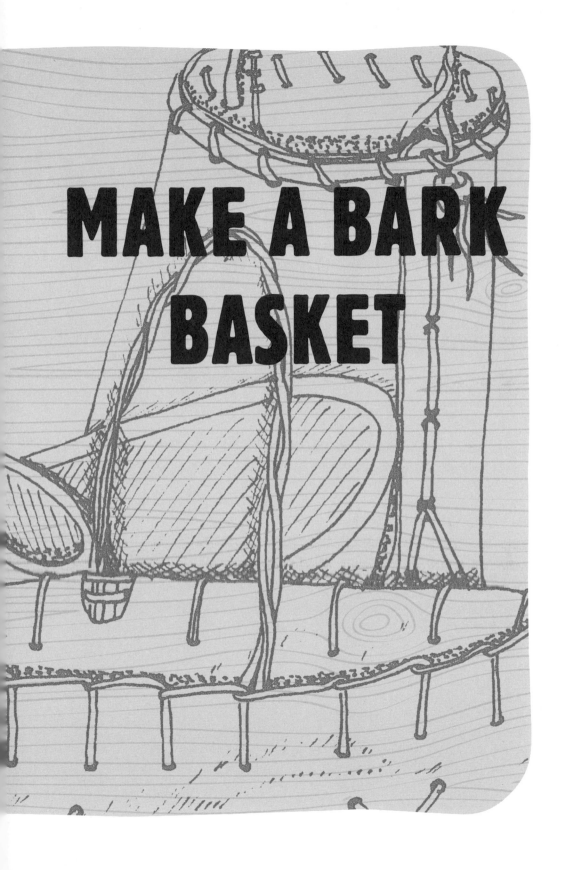

MAKE A BARK BASKET

Imagine a life without plastic leftovers containers. I'm not sure it would be bearable, but somehow, our ancestors managed. One of the ways they did it was by making all kinds of baskets. A bark basket is a quick and easy container solution.

▲▲▲ MAKE A BARK BASKET

Find a tree that has fallen over. Cut a piece of bark from the trunk that is a long rectangular shape with corners that flare outward on the longer edges. If you don't flare the edges, the opening of your basket will be smaller than you want it to be and harder to get things in and out of. You want the length of the rectangle to be about three times longer than the width.

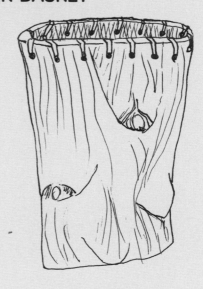

TYPES OF BARK

If the tree fell over recently, you'll have to pry the outer bark off the trunk once you've cut the shape you want. If it has been on the ground for a long time, you might find the bark is quite dry; however, you can still use this bark if you soak the piece you cut in water for a while. Some tree barks work really well for this project, and others don't work at all. Depending on where you live, **birch** (northern states), **tulip tree** (Southeast), **silver maple** (Midwest), and **cedar** (many regions) are the kinds you'll want to look for.

SCORE THE BARK

Take your stone knife and use the sharp edge to score the outline of the flared rectangular shape. Don't try to cut through the bark all at once. Make a light outline score first, and then go round and round the outline, cutting in a little deeper each time you go around. If you try to cut through all at once, the pressure against the curve of the bark, or where it releases from the trunk, is likely to crack the bark. You are going to do your best to remove the flared rectangle of bark from the trunk in one whole, uncracked piece. You can repair cracks with pitch glue and lacing, but it's easier and quicker if you don't have to.

QUESTION

Is the bark pliable? Once you have the rectangle cut, check that it is supple enough to bend, either because it is fresh or because you soaked it long enough. Some barks need to be soaked even if they are fresh. When you can bend the bark without cracking or breaking, you want to make a score in the shape of an eye right in the middle of the rectangle, going across the short width of the rectangle.

SCORE AN EYE IN THE CENTER

First lay the inner side of the bark down on a flat surface. Use a piece of charcoal on the outer side of the bark to make a straight line from side to side (the shortest distance) to mark the exact center. Now, make the shape of a human eye with that line as your guide to make each side of the eye equal. Score this eye shape slowly, making the outline first. Go a little deeper each time you trace the outline. Do not

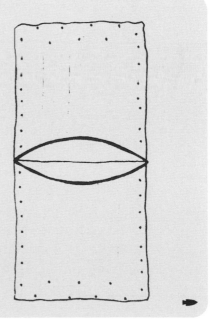

score the centerline! You do not want the bottom of your basket to fold. Make this eye-shaped score about halfway through the bark. You want to be able to bend the ends upward at this score, but you don't want to cut all the way through.

MAKE HOLES WITH A BONE AWL
Now, using an awl (see Make a Bone Knife or Awl, p. 209) or drill tip, make holes along each long edge of the bark. These holes will hold the plant fiber string (see Make String and Rope from Plant Fibers, p. 15) as you stitch the two sides together. By measuring the same distance between each hole, you can have the holes match each other when you fold up the edges, or you can place the holes in an alternating pattern. Now, make two lines of holes on both of the shorter edges. These holes will hold the stitching that secures the top edging trim.

STITCH THE SIDES
Check that the bark is still pliable and folds up easily without crack-ing. Take your handmade string, or any other lacing you are planning to use, and stitch the sides of your

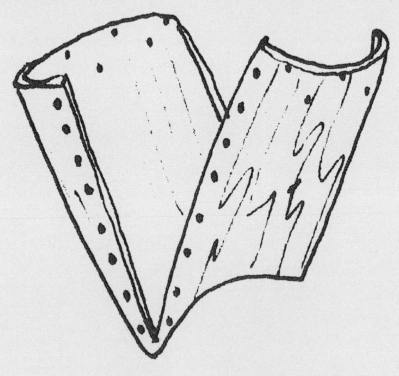

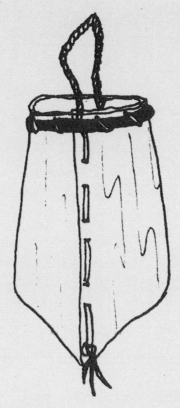

bark basket. Start your stitching at the center score on one side, stitch up that whole side, leave a big length of string at the top, and then go down the other side; tie a knot there to finish. The loop of string you left over the top will be a carrying loop. You can make your stitches in an X pattern by going up once and back down, or you can double up the lacing by going several times.

TRIM THE TOP

You can make a trim piece for the top out of a small strip of the bark you used for the basket body, or out of another bark of a different color. Stitch it to the holes that you already made along the top edge. A large piece of string or rope that you made with plant fiber can make a nice trim, or a colorful strip of cloth works well. Try splitting a small green branch or willow branch in half and applying the flat inner edge against the outer bark of the basket. So many choices!

MAKE A ROPE COIL BASKET

A coiled basket is another kind of basket that is easy to make. To make a coiled basket means that you take a long strand of some kind of material and spiral it around itself, stitching each coil to the coil below as you go. If you wanted a flat platter, you wouldn't bend each coil upward as you stitch. If you want a bowl, you will gently elevate each coil as you go. For a basket, you'll make the bottom flat and set each coil directly on top of the next one, all the way up to the height you desire.

It's a very simple technique, but becoming consistent takes time. However, once you have the technique down, you'll have a more beautiful finished product.

▲▲▲
TO MAKE THE BASKET

GATHER MATERIALS

First, you need to find the material you want to coil. This really could be just about anything: rope, strips of cloth (think rag rug), long pine needles, hair, seaweed, twisted cattail leaves, or whatever you can find that is flexible enough to coil up and sturdy enough to be stitched.

PREPARE MATERIALS

If you need to prepare the material in some way before you coil it, like making it into string or rope,

do that ahead of time and have it ready. Then decide what kind of material you will use for the stitching thread, like string, strips of **dog bane** fiber, or the long, thin inner pieces from a **yucca** leaf. Prepare a good amount of that stitching material.

USE A BONE AWL FOR STITCHING

If the coil materials are somewhat large and rather loose and your stitching material has a firmness to it, you can use your bone awl to push an area open in the coil and put your stitching material through by hand.

USE A TAPESTRY NEEDLE AND BONE AWL
If the coil and stitching material is relatively fine, it will help to have a large-eyed tapestry needle to stitch with. The points of these needles are pretty blunt, so if you need to use your bone to poke a hole through the coil material first, that might be helpful

TECHNIQUE OPTIONS
You can do your stitching by going all the way around two coils at a time to secure them together or by penetrating through the center of the coils. Alternatively, you can stitch from either the inside or the outside of the basket so that the stitching only shows on one side.

DESIGN OPTIONS
Once you get consistent and can hold the coils in a good shape, you may want to take the time to stitch fancy designs as you go. You can use colored plant materials for the coil or the stitching to give contrast, or you can dye the fibers of your coil material and put patterns into your baskets.

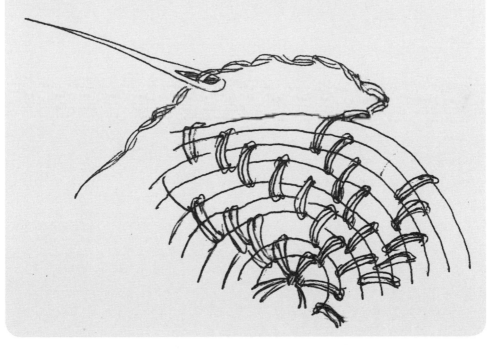

apple

MAKE COUGH SYRUP WITH MEDICINAL PLANTS

Comforting and effective medicines are all around us in urban, country, and wilderness environments. Many of the wild plants we use as foods support our well-being and can also have very effective medicinal benefits. When you begin incorporating wild foods into your diet, your body systems respond with improved health and energy. Your food is your medicine, then, and less often do you feel the need for stronger medicinal preparations.

ROLE MODELING

Children respond well to herbal preparations. If you've ever been in the position of having to give a child something like cough syrup, you know the experience can be more traumatic for you than the child. Involving young ones in the collection and preparation of the plants to make syrups and lotions that will calm and soothe them seems to have a magical effect on their willingness to apply or ingest these preparations. Many of the plants we use for skin or lip care, cuts

and bruises, and soothing throat preparations are so beautiful. Collecting them is pure pleasure, and it's a rare child who doesn't like to be up on the step stool helping cut, pound, mix, and bubble and boil away.

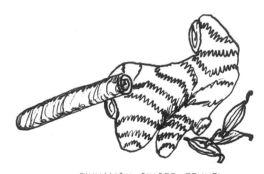

CINNAMON, GINGER, FENNEL

CONSIDER

Earlier, when we were talking about cooking on the fire, that idea of children being a part of the whole process came up. Involving children in the process of creating tonics and syrups creates lots of "buy-in" when it's time to swallow something. Applying balms and salves to owies is a little easier when you've made them yourself, when the plant is your friend, and when your name, in your own writing, is on the little jar of unction.

MAKE COUGH SYRUP

Licorice root helps coughs. I like to chew on the root, but most young ones find this too strong. A syrup is much more palatable for them. I mentioned Rosemary Gladstar's plant book in Gather Wild Food in the City, p. 57. For years I have followed her instructions for the combination of herbs that makes good cough syrup.

1 quart water

4 parts fennel seed

2 parts licorice root

2 parts slippery elm bark

2 parts valerian

2 parts wild cherry bark

1 part cinnamon stick

1/2 part ginger root

1/8 part orange peel

1/2 cup grade A dark color/robust flavor maple syrup

1/2 (12-ounce) container frozen apple juice concentrate

Decide how much fennel seed you want to use according to your taste and then adjust the other herb amounts accordingly. I suggest starting with 1/2 cup fennel seed.

Put the water in a heavy-bottomed pot. Add the herbs. Simmer this tea on a low heat until the liquid is reduced by half. Pour the mixture into a jar and let it sit for about 1 hour. Pour the tea through a strainer back into the pot. Add the maple syrup and apple juice. Stir everything together over a low heat until the syrup and juice concentrate is well combined. Do not boil. Pour the liquid back into the jar. Take 1 to 2 teaspoons every hour or whenever you have a fit of coughing. The cough syrup can be stored in the refrigerator for several weeks.

Depending on where you live, some of these ingredients would be difficult to find in the woods. However, none of them are difficult to find in supermarkets with an herbal section.

MAKE
HEALING
SALVES

These herbs make a comforting salve for scrapes, rashes, cuts, and other skin irritations: **comfrey** flowers, leaves, and roots, **calendula** flowers, and **St. John's wort** flowers.

Comfrey can be found growing wild in many places. Calendula is easy to find in garden centers and easy to grow; it is often used in landscaping across urban areas. St. John's wort flowers can be gathered and dried, or they can be purchased at supermarkets that have an herb section.

▲▲▲
MAKE A SALVE

Using the sun to infuse the oil for salve making takes about 1 month.

GATHER AND PREPARE THE HERBS

Comfrey flowers, leaves, and roots

Calendula flowers

St. John's wort flowers

Rose petals (optional)

2 (1-quart) canning jars

Pure olive oil

Cheesecloth

Beeswax

Several small tins or salve
  containers

Collect and dry the herbs. Cut the stem and leaves at the base of the plant and gather into bundles. Tie cotton or linen string around the stems and hang the bundle in a cool dark area. Split the comfrey root into long, thin pieces to dry, and then grind into a powder. Combine the dried herbs into a 10-ounce mix of equal parts. I also like to add dried rose petals. Put 5 ounces of this mix in a canning jar. Put the other 5 ounces in another canning jar and set it aside for later.

PREPARE THE HERB-INFUSED OIL

Fill the first jar with olive oil. Set that jar in a warm, sunny spot for 2 weeks.

After 2 weeks, take the second jar with the other 5 ounces of the herb mixture and put a piece of cheesecloth over the jar, making a small depression in the center of the cloth, and secure it to the outer edge of the jar with a rubber band. Pour the oil from the first jar into the second jar. Wrap the oily herbs from the first jar in a little ball with the cheesecloth and squeeze out any remaining oil into the new jar. Let this jar sit in the sun for 2 more weeks.

Use the cheesecloth to strain the herb-infused oil into a container.

PREPARE THE SALVE

Pour half of the strained oil into a heavy-bottomed pot, and warm it gently over a very low heat. Grate 1/4 cup beeswax into the warm oil. After the beeswax melts, transfer a little bit of the salve to a saucer, and place it in the refrigerator for just a few minutes. If it sets up very hard, not viscous enough for salve, you can add a little more of your oil to the pot. If your test puddle is too runny, add a little more beeswax instead.

FILL THE TINS OR CONTAINERS

When the unguent is smooth and spreadable, a consistency that you like, pour the warm mix from the pot into the containers. If you keep this happy healing balm in a cool, dark place, it can last a long time, even for years.

FOR THE LITTLE ONES

This herb salve also makes nice lip balm and heals chapping. Give each of the young ones their very own container, and let them put their name and draw a picture on the lid. The next time they get a scrape or cut, they'll be happy to dip a finger in their own little salve pot instead of running down the street screaming bloody murder as you chase them with a tube of Neosporin.

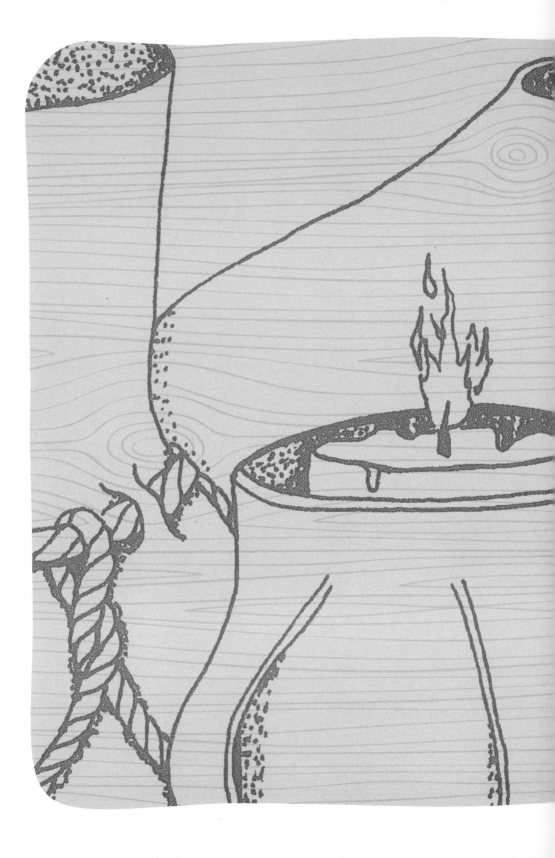

MAKE A LAMP AND CANDLES

Fat burns. No, this is not the name of the latest rage exercise program. It is simply a statement. Long ago, our ancestors made little stone lamps out of animal fat. This is a fun project, and you'll be surprised how long the light from a little pile of animal fat and a handmade plant wick will last.

KNOWLEDGE

Rendering a substance means cooking it down to reduce its volume and separate any impurities that promote spoilage. Lard is rendered animal fat. Butter is rendered to make ghee, removing the cream content from the butter. Shortening is the vegetable equivalent of lard; it's like whipped oil. All of these products last a long time without refrigeration. Oil burns too. Fashionable home stores sell candles that are simply containers of oil with floating wicks. Back in the day, our ancestors used fat to make light, before they learned to press oil from plant seed.

♠♠ RENDER THE FAT

You could go buy a pound of lard, or you can learn the skill of rendering to make your own lard. If you're a hunter, save the fat from the animal you harvest. Otherwise, save fat scraps from raw meat you prepare. Freeze the scraps until you have enough to fill a jar with lard. To render the fat down into a clean liquid form, slowly heat small chunks over a very low flame. The smaller you cut up the fat, the more quickly it will liquefy. Skim off any of the bits that don't turn to liquid.

DRY THE JARS AND LIDS

Get some clean, sterilized canning jars, make sure they are completely dry inside, and pour the liquefied fat into the jars, leaving about 1 inch of room under the lid. Put the clean, dry lids on right away.

STORAGE

Set these jars in a cool, dark place, and this fat will stay fresh and usable for a very long time. Rendered lard can last for years when properly stored.

USES

It can be used for frying other foods; making pie crust, biscuits, pemmican (a sort of ancestral jerky), or cattail night torches; waterproofing leather shoes; or for making fat lamps, which we're going to do right now.

▲▲▲
MAKE A FAT LAMP

Find a soft rock like soapstone, sandstone, or limestone. Flatten the bottom by rubbing back and forth on a coarse stone, like a sandstone slab, or a sidewalk. Do this so the rock sits without tipping over. Grind out the middle with a harder rock until you have a small well in the center. If you can't find a rock to shape, you could use a seashell instead. Any bowl-like container that won't burn will work. If you're an exuberant recycler, use a tuna can, or get an even taller food can and poke holes in a pattern all around the top half.

MAKE THE WICK

Use plant fiber to make a string about as thick as a candlewick. Before you begin to twist the two sides around each other, take a little bit of the animal fat and grease up the full length of plant fiber. You will have a fat-coated wick that will stay lit and burn well.

POUR FAT INTO STONE CONTAINER

Fill the well of your stone or shell lamp with rendered fat. Keep the fat level below the edge of the well. As the fat burns, it will liquefy, so if you fill the well too full, it will spill out of the stone container.

PLACE THE WICK

Poke the wick straight down into the center of the fat with a skinny stick. Now light the top tip of the wick on fire.

IDEA

You can make several of these and take them to your special spot out in the woods. Set some stumps around your little area, and place a fat lamp on each one. It's a magical way to spend a dark evening in the woods. It's also a nice way to have a little firelight if you're in an area where it isn't safe to make a fire.

NOTE

Store your lamp in a closed container. If there is fat left in the well, critters will come and eat the fat at night. If you're in an area where there are dogs, bears, or rodents, you'll want to be careful not to spill any of the fat while you're using the lamps. Fat is a tasty, tempting treat no matter who—or what—you are!

▲▲▲ MAKE CANDLES

You can use the same plant-fiber wicks to make candles at home with old crayons and/or household wax. I rub the plant fiber with animal fat before I twist the fiber into a wick, like we did with the lamp. Use an old Crock-Pot to melt the crayons and/or wax. Take a stick and, holding it horizontally, tie two or three wicks across it, close enough together to fit into the Crock-Pot.

BUILD UP THE WAX ON THE WICK

Dip the wicks straight down into the melted wax, and lift the stick straight out. Your candles will be as long as the depth of your melted wax. Dip down slowly so that the wicks stay straight and then lift out right away. If you leave the growing candles down in the melted wax too long, the wax will melt off the wick faster than it will build up. In between each step, hold the stick up in the air for a moment to allow the new layer of wax to solidify.

TAPERED TOPS

Continue dipping the wicks until the candles are as thick as you want them to be. As each layer of wax builds up, the wax level in the Crock-Pot lowers. This will give your dipped candle a naturally tapered top.

MOLDED CANDLES

You can also make an earth-molded candle with your plant-fiber wick and melted wax. Again, make your plant fiber wick and melt the wax. Dig a hole in the sandbox or any outside area with sandy soil. Get the sand wet so that the sides of the shape you dig don't cave in. For extra decoration, you can line the hole with different leaves or sparkly diatomaceous earth or glitter before you pour the wax in.

Tie your wick to a stick, and then set the stick across the opening of the little shape you dug so that the wick is directly in the center and hangs to the bottom. Now carefully pour the hot wax into your little earth mold. When the wax cools and hardens all the way through, you can take your molded candle out of the ground and brush the sand and dirt away. Cool, huh?

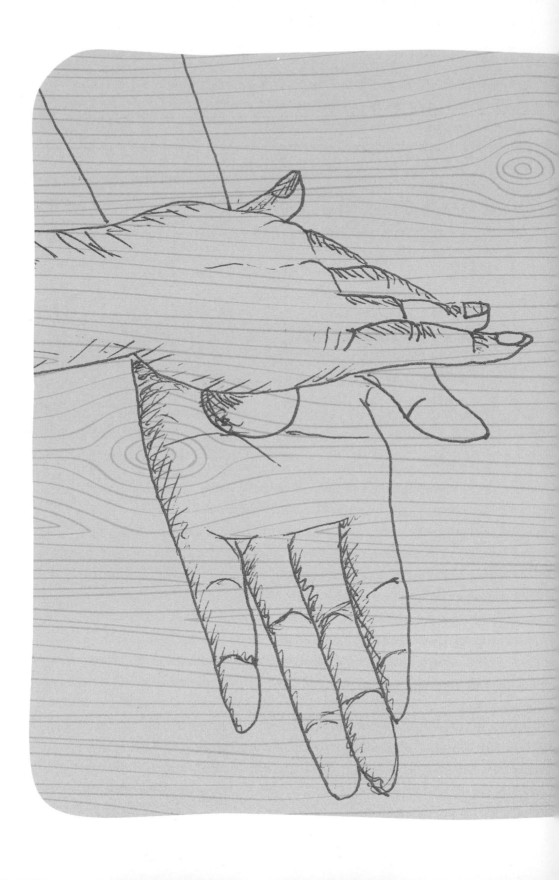

MAKE FELT BALLS AND OTHER TOYS

Did you get a good feel for how felting works in Make Felted Material from Natural Fibers, p. 119? A fun and easy felt project to start with is making a felt ball.

MAKE A FELT BALL

Grab a handful of your raw fiber and wad it up in your fist. Pull out long wisps of fiber and wrap the wad tightly. Wrap these wisps of fiber around and around the wad like you are winding up a ball of yarn. Continue to wrap the forming ball in all different directions until it fills both of your hands. It is important to keep the ball tight as you wrap so that the finished ball doesn't have a lot of air pockets inside and a wrinkled cover on the outside.

WET AND WORK THE BALL OF FIBER

Fill a bucket or a bowl with hot water. Rub your palms and fingers with a thin coating of soap. Grab the ball in both hands and plunge it into the water. Start rubbing the wet ball with your soapy hands all over and around, applying inward pressure. As the wet ball cools off, plunge it back into the hot water. If the fibers begin to stick to your hands as you work the ball, add a little more soap to your palms. The ball will start to shrink, and at some point, you'll shrink it down as far as it will go.

WEIGHT THE BALLS

The size of the ball is determined by the shrinkage rate of the fiber and how much you wrap around before you begin the felting process. You can make a fairly large ball, and it will actually be pretty lightweight when it dries. These are great balls for babies and toddlers, and they make fun ornaments during the holidays. If you're going to use the balls in some kind of game, you can add more weight so they move more accurately or rapidly. Add a round, heavy object to the center, like some kind of large metal bearing.

MAKE A COLOR-LAYERED BALL THAT OPENS AND CLOSES

COLOR-LAYER BALL

Try this fun toy. Choose a brightly colored fiber, and make the wad and the first several inches of wrap from that same color. Next, choose another bright, contrasting color and wrap with several inches of that color. Make five or six layers in bright, contrasting colors. Follow the description above to finish felting the ball. Once it dries, take a very sharp knife and cut the ball in half. You'll see all the beautiful rings of bright colors.

MAKE THE HINGES

Take a little rectangular scrap of leather or fabric and sew it onto the outside edges of both halves of the ball, holding the two halves together while you sew. Just make your stitches on the outside of the

halves so that when you're done, you can open the two halves and see the inside of each one.

ADD THE CLOSURE

Now take a button and stitch it at the edge of one of the halves on the opposite side from your hands. Make a little string from leather lacing or plant fiber, and sew a little loop onto the other half. You can close the ball and play with it by looping the button. Then, you can open it up and look at the pretty colors inside.

MAKE A FELTED DOLL OR ANIMAL

When we first described how to felt, we mentioned that whatever direction you rub the fiber in is the direction in which it will shrink. Because of this, you can make all kinds of three-dimensional figures. To make a felted doll, take some fiber, wad it up, and wrap it in a small head-shaped ball. Next, make a short, fat hot dog shape for the body. Make four more short, chubby hot dog shapes for the arms and legs. Use wisps of fiber to wrap the entire figure into one piece. You can place the arms and legs in any positions you want to imitate motion, sitting, swimming, or whatever you want. Once you have the figure wrapped, shrink it down just like you did the ball. Of course, you could make animals instead of people or anything else you can think of. Have fun!

MAKE FELT WITH CONTRASTING COLOR PATTERNS

APPLY PATTERNS TO YOUR FELT

You can make designs in flat felt using multiple colors. For your first try, choose two contrasting colors like white and black. Lay up one of the colors in a big square. See Make Felted Material from Natural Fibers, p. 119, if you need to refresh your memory on how to do this.

APPLY THE CONTRAST

Once the felt is as thick as you want, take the second color and begin to lay it on the top in a pattern that you want. Let's say you choose a circle. You are going to pull out little wisps of the second color and lay them into that shape, just as if you were painting them on. Remember to lay the little bits of fiber in varying directions. It takes some time and practice to get shaped edges clean and defined. Sometimes I use a fork or a little pokey stick to help set the contrasting fibers into place.

APPLY THE WATER

Instead of dribbling the hot water all over the fiber like you did when you followed the set of directions in Make Felted Material from Natural Fibers, dribble the water onto the contrasting color first, setting it down into place before you do the rest of the edges.

START FINGERTIPPING

Use your soapy fingers to fingertip it down into place. The rest of the felting process is the same, but you concentrate on gently coaxing the pattern to grip into the under layer, usually with a little more fingertipping and an even softer initial rubbing back and forth before the fiber skins up.

BE CREATIVE

When you get good at this, you can actually felt panels of whole landscapes, like a painting, or any kinds of designs you want.

FIND YOUR WAY USING NATURE'S SIGNPOSTS

As we spend more time playing in the woods, we see patterns all around us. I love noticing the way so many things mimic each other, and I guess it makes sense when everything, including us, is being formed, shaped, and changed by the same natural forces. There are frost patterns that look just like the intricate layout of feathers in an eagle's wing. There are overlapping wave patterns in solid, sun-baked red rock that are identical to the surface ripples in the flowing, muddy red river water between those rock banks. There are mushroom caps with intricate shingled patterns that look exactly like the shell of an armadillo.

KNOWLEDGE
WIND SHAPING
One of the nature patterns you can use for wayfinding is seen in the way the trees grow. Trees that are flexible and sway in the breeze, like cottonwoods, willows, and birch, will list leeward when exposed to constant wind. They will have a bend as if still being pushed by the wind, even when it is not blowing.

Trees that are rigid and do not sway will have less branches on the windward side of the trunk than they do on the leeward side. Sometimes this is very obvious, like when you're wandering about in the high alpine zones of our tallest mountains, on windy coastlines, or if you're out in the middle of the great prairies and plains. Even in more sheltered conditions, you will begin to notice that an area that has consistent winds will usually have trees and bushes with more branches on the leeward side.

If you're spending time in a particular area, these patterns will help you know what to expect when the wind does begin to blow. Moreover, if you know the general wind direction of an area, these patterns will help you determine cardinal direction. This would be most useful to you if you have an idea of which direction you are trying to go.

TACTILE CLUES IN SNOW

Wild winter winds in the area around us often create blizzard situations. In a blizzard, it is very hard to tell cardinal directions, and predominant wind patterns are often overcome by wild little vortexes when the wind meets obstacles. It's also hard to see anything at all. Before the snow piles up too much, you can get a sense of which direction you are traveling in by using this crunchy snow trick: Where the sunshine melts the snow and then re-freezes again at night, a hard, crunchy crust develops on the top of the snow that is very different from the snow in the areas where the sun doesn't shine. Go on outside and stomp around a little while through the snowy woods. It won't take long for you to hear and feel the difference in the snow on the south side of a tree compared to the snow on the north side, where the sun isn't shining. This can be a helpful way to determine direction.

VISUAL CLUES IN SNOW

Remember how we talked about energy moving in waves? (See Make a Stone Knife, p. 27.) Wind makes wave patterns in snow. If you know the prevailing winds in your area, you can look at snowdrifts to get a sense of direction. The higher, steeper angle will usually be facing the direction the wind is blowing from. The wind hits up against a small obstacle on the ground and swirls back on itself like a curling wave in the ocean, dumping snow on the windward side of the drift before sloping back down the other side and moving along. If you're going to pitch some kind of shelter in winter weather or dig into a drift for shelter, it's good to know. You'll want to thoughtfully consider where you place the opening to your shelter so that you don't get buried in.

SUN INFLUENCE

Plants can also be an indicator of direction. Flowering plants often have the face of their flowers pointed toward the sunniest part of the sky. **Sunflowers** are the classic example. The reason we call them sunflowers is because the face of the flower is continually pointing toward the sun. If you didn't actually know this before, it's really fun to go check it out. In the morning, the fuzzy brown center of the flower will be facing east; by the evening, it will have turned to face the west. If you happen to be cast adrift in the great prairies of Kansas, this is going to be a very useful piece of information.

In his amazing volume of woods lore, *Wildwood Wisdom*, Ellsworth Jaeger writes about the tips of pine and hemlock, which almost always nod in an easterly direction.

CENTRIFUGE EFFECT

Here in the northern hemisphere, another wonderful thing that plants do is spiral upwards in a counter-clockwise direction. Dust devils, hurricanes, and whirlpools in rivers, along with the climbing plants, chase the same path the earth is taking every day. If you stick your finger straight up in the air and imitate the spiral of a climbing vine you find in the woods, you know that your finger will be moving from east to north to west to south, again and again, as you trace that spiral.

IDEA

Did you ever wonder why so many of us are right-handed? After all, if you were a climbing plant, your right side would be your leading edge. I wonder if there's anything to that idea.

KNOWLEDGE

SUMMER TACTILE AND VISUAL CLUES

In summer months, wayfinding methods might include watching for patches of moss. Where I live, it can be quite dry, and ground moss can only be found in the environment it needs: the shady north side of the trees, where the moist soil is. At high altitude, the sun is very intense, and the trunks of many trees have lighter bark on their south side, where they are constantly exposed to bleaching ultraviolet rays. Each area and region has its own unique features and responses to everything that happens in, on, and around it. The more time you spend in the woods, the more familiar you will become with the wayfinding signposts of nature.

MAKE COLORFUL DYES AND STAINS FROM PLANTS

We talked about making earth mineral pigments to stain and paint in Make Your Own Paints with Earth Minerals, p. 145. Besides the rocks, soils, and clays that give us so many amazing colors, plants are also a resource for beautiful dyes and stains.

KNOWLEDGE

When making plant dyes, it is not always the whole plant that needs to be used. Sometimes the root of the plant is where the color is, or perhaps it is in the flower. Some plant parts give up their color by simply soaking them in water. Others have to be processed with other resources or cooked down to release the best color.

There are lots of really good resources for becoming knowledgeable about making plant dye. Any good fiber shop will carry a good supply of dye materials and have many plant dye books to learn from. (See Resources, p. 302.)

KNOWLEDGE
KEEPING THE COLOR

When you immerse cloth, leather, or fibers you have felted or spun into a dye bath, you can get a really beautiful color. It might last a long time, it might only last until you wash it, or it might fade with the sun. Certain additions to the dye bath can help set the color in the material so that it will have staying power. Many liquids and powdered minerals work as mordants, change agents that set the dye color. You can use the same dye plant and add it to different kinds of mordants, getting completely different colors.

DYE PLANTS

In addition to the flowers and leaves that you would expect to make good dyes, many lichens and mushrooms also make good dye plants, and many trees grow fruits, nuts, or seeds that give good dye. The spring buds of the **narrowleaf**

cottonwood make a beautiful purple stain, and you can also boil the buds down to make a fixative for other pigments. Many berries can be used as stains. You only have to make a big mash out of them and press the juices. Add a little vinegar to the juice before you use the stain, and you'll get some interesting color variations as well as a longer-lasting stain. Berry stain is fun for face paint too!

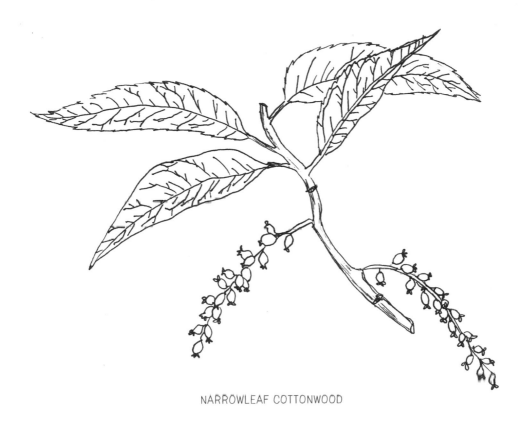

NARROWLEAF COTTONWOOD

MAKE A DYE BATH

A really easy dye to make and use is **black walnut** dye. Black walnuts are available in many varying environments. In the latter part of the growing season, the internal nut and its hard, corrugated shell are encased in a thick, round husk that has a light avocado-green color. Although the nutshell itself gives off some dye, it is the spongy interior of the husk that gives the strongest dye.

COLLECT AND SOAK

Collect whatever you can, and then crack the nuts open and split the outer greenish husk into pieces.

Cover it all with water, put a lid on it, and forget about it. Over several weeks or months, it can sit and wait. One fall I made a bucket of dye and forgot all about it. In the below-freezing temperatures the following winter, the bottom of the bucket split and cracked when the dye liquid froze. I didn't notice. Later in the spring, a beautiful black puddle of liquid seeped out into the ground. Years later, that area of the ground is still very stained and dark, and insects avoid it! (That might be good to know.) I put the thawed mess of hull and husk into another bucket, added

BLACK WALNUTS

more water, waited another month, and still got a beautiful dye bath.

MAKE DYE WITH A MORDANT

Osage orange is a tree that grows great bow staves. We do a lot of bow making here at Earth Knack, and I gather up all the shavings and soak them in a bucket, just like I described with black walnut. The color I get from these shavings is lovely, but it doesn't last long after washing. Since iron acts as a mordant, I add a bunch of rusty hardware to the bucket. I usually simmer this dye bath down, reducing it to half its volume, before use; then the color lasts well.

TIE-DYE YOUR WHITE T-SHIRT

Take one of your all-cotton white T-shirts and twist up handfuls of the fabric, securing the twist with rubber bands, just like you would for any tie-dye project. Put the shirt into your prepared bucket of dye. Let it sit for several hours. The longer it sits, the better the color pattern will show. Once the fabric looks like the right darkness to you, pull the shirt out of the dye, and without removing the rubber bands, let it dry out. Then remove the rubber bands. Rinse the shirt once to get out the wrinkles and let it dry again.

HOW TO BOIL WATER IN THE WOODS

Water is life. As the old first aid and survival adage goes, you can live three minutes without air, three days without water, and three weeks without food.

CONSIDER

These three essential commodities—air, water, food—should be the ones that we cherish, collect, use, and experience with the utmost reverence. Curious, then, that participating in modern living systems has made such a dirty mess of all three. It is so heartening to see all the effort being put into clean air, water, and food over the last few decades. Only a few decades before this, there wasn't even a collective consciousness about the need to keep these things clean. This shift in our thinking makes me hopeful that we will find more solutions for integrating our modern lifestyle choices with respect for resource use.

KNOWLEDGE

Clean water is essential to our well-being. Almost everybody has heard that if you boil water that isn't healthy to drink, it will usually be purified and safe for drinking.

PURIFICATION METHODS

Boiling water requires a fuel source, which is not always available, but chemical treatments (like iodine), filtration pump systems, or more recent ultraviolet purification technology can be carried along on any jaunt. Iodine tablets can be purchased at any pharmacy, and other filtration systems can be found at outdoor and sports stores.

HARD TIMES

Sometimes, though, you are just plain out of options. If you can't make a solar still to distill some fresh water from the moisture of plants around you (see Survival Shelters, p. 183), you need to figure out how to boil up some water to make it safe to drink. Part of the trouble you run into in a survival situation is having a container that can hold the water while it boils. If you carry a metal water bottle in your carry-along bag (and you've remembered to bring it along), you've got that problem solved.

BE PREPARED

A nice little trick to be prepared for emergencies is to carry a good-size sheet of heavy-duty aluminum foil. This sheet weighs next to nothing and folds up small. You can stick it in a pocket or add it to your carry-along bag. When you need to boil some water, you can shape it into a container and set it right on the fire.

KNOWLEDGE

Even if you have a pot, boiling water on a fire is not always as easy as it sounds. The biggest mistake most of us make when boiling water or cooking liquid on the fire is not thoughtfully securing the pot. It isn't something we usually need to think about, so it almost always catches us by surprise when our pot tips over and spills its contents. This actually happens fairly often.

You can usually set a pot fairly securely on a pile of burning sticks. The trouble starts when the sticks burn up and start to change shape. There is nothing predictable about a pile of burning sticks; they all burn up and shift in different ways at different times. Vigilance is the price of an unspilled pot.

COMMON SENSE

This sounds too simple, like common sense, but if you're not thinking about it, you won't get the water. Common sense is earned; it's not inherent. It always makes me smile when someone says, "Why don't you just use your common sense?" and they are talking about something you have absolutely no experience with.

After you get some experience, you might figure out that you can build up a ring of burning wood around the container. As the wood underneath the container burns away, the outer ring of sticks will create some support for the pot, so when it tips a little, it won't tip over. As the ring of sticks burns, just keep adding a few more, and you will have the support you need for the pot throughout the boiling process.

USE STUFF AROUND THE HOUSE TO MAKE FIRE

Where there's smoke, is there fire? Well, not always. So it is a really great idea to have a big bag of fire-making tricks. There are all kinds of things around that you can start a fire with.

MAKE A FIRE WITH A MAGNIFYING GLASS

Most of us are familiar with the magnifying-glass trick. If you're not, go out on a sidewalk or other place where you can put a crumpled pile of dried leaves or bits of dried plant that will catch fire easily without catching fire to whatever you have placed them on!

Now, take a quick look at where the sun is, and place your magnifying glass between the sun and the pile of dried tinder. Turn the glass so that one side of the lens is facing straight toward the sunlight and the other side of the lens is facing the tinder.

Because the lens is convex (meaning that it arches slightly upward across the surface), it will focus the sunlight coming in on one side into a small, targeted ray going out the other side. You want to direct that light ray right into your tinder pile.

This sounds simple, but it isn't that easy to hold the lens steady and direct the light with pinpoint accuracy onto the tinder. You need to be very accurate because an amazing amount of heat is being generated when the sunlight passes through the lens. It is this heat that is allowing combustion to happen. If you wiggle it all around, one particular spot can't get hot enough to combust.

CONSIDER

It's funny how when you're just messing around with the magnifying glass, you can catch all kinds of things on fire. When you decide you want fire, or if you're thinking you really need one, it suddenly becomes a lot more difficult to do. The anxiousness we feel often prevents us from doing the exact thing we are trying to do. That's what makes practice such a good thing. Practiced technique is your automatic override for jittery performance. When you know that you know a thing, the certainty inside you doesn't go away, even if you're not doing it very well at the moment.

MAKE A PARABOLA FIRE

You need to get a dished, concave reflective piece of material and put very dry, fine tinder in the bottom. There are still a lot of old cars and trucks around with the big, round headlights. If you can get a hold of one of these, you can use it to start a fire. The part you need is the inside shiny, reflective part that is shaped like a bulging megaphone. It has a small hole in the lower center where the headlamp bulb sits. Round flashlights with the old-style bulb in the middle have the same shape and can be used the same way.

The magnifying lens has a convex surface. The headlight container has a concave surface; this means the center of the surface drops inward. This shape allows sunlight to get focused down into the center hole when you point the bulb casing directly at the sun. This is the same principle used in solar-oven production. If you hold some very fine, dry tinder right in the center where the little light bulb used to be, that tinder will combust.

Remember that piece of tinfoil you might have packed in your carry-along bag (see Survival Shelters, p. 183)? You can make a wide foil funnel and use it to start your fire. The less wrinkled the foil is, the better it will concentrate the heat. Why? Because the wrinkles have a whole bunch of different angled surfaces, all reflecting the light to other places besides the very center bottom of the funnel. That sends the light and the heat in all different directions. If you can't concentrate the heat in one little place, you won't achieve combustion.

MAKE A
FLINT AND
STEEL FIRE

Flint and steel fire making was very popular in the mountain man and pioneer days. Blacksmithing was an established art, and metal strikers could be forged and easily carried.

Wandering about through the hills, plains, and mountains, it is easy to find chips and flakes of flint. Ancestral people have made stone tools and weapons for tens of thousands of years, and bits and pieces of these past activities are scattered across the land. Many regions have natural deposits of agate, flint, and chert, which strike wonderful sparks when knocked against a piece of steel that has lower carbon content than stainless steel or alloyed blades.

FIND FLINT AND STEEL TO STRIKE SPARKS

GATHER YOUR STEEL AND FLINT
I keep extolling the virtues of the Old Hickory knife, and if you have been persuaded to get your own, pull it out now to practice making flint and steel sparks. If I'm going to have to continue badgering you about getting one of these knives for yourself, you can use any little scrap chunk of metal that has a low carbon content.

Basic steel is a mix of iron and carbon. As the carbon content rises, the metal sparks better. Sparks that spray out in long filaments and travel downward are best for flint and steel.

Most metal folks use for flint and steel has enough carbon to strike sparks that go out in all directions like a firecracker. If you choose a metal with just a little lower carbon content, like the Old Hickory knife, you get the longer sparks that direct right into your tinder.

If you choose too low a carbon content, you won't get any sparks.

Most tool and utensil metals are steel alloyed with other metals or stainless. These don't spark either.

Once you have the metal, find a piece of flint that has a thin, sharp edge. You will strike a sharp edge of the metal (or the blunt back end, not the cutting edge, of your Old Hickory knife) against the sharp edge of the flint. The thinner the edges of the flint are, the better sparks you'll get.

NOTE

Stainless steel and most household tools like screwdrivers, wrenches, and hammers are not made of low-carbon metal stock. Blades from old-fashioned lawnmowers, scrap pieces from the chassis of older vehicles, or old metal porch and stairway railings can make good sparks.

QUESTION

Why does a thin edge make a difference? Because this striking creates friction, friction creates heat, and heat transfers most easily to the thinnest edges. Voila! Sparks!

SAFETY

You are going to strike the blunt side of your knife against the flint. This means the sharp edge will be facing your palm. Remember how we mentioned in Safe Handling of Tools and Knives, p. 39, that there are times when you might hold the sharp edge of a knife toward yourself? This is one of those times. While you are not applying pressure and moving the blade toward yourself, you still need to be very careful to hold the metal blade firmly. For extra safety, it's a good idea to wear a tough leather glove. Hold the handle of the knife downward so that the weight of the handle is easier to support as you strike.

PRACTICE STRIKING SPARKS

Firmly hold the flint edge horizontally in one hand. Hold the metal edge vertically in the other hand. Strike the metal downward across the flint edge. Hold the metal high and strike down quickly. Follow through the full strike. Sometimes you get sparks on the first strike, and sometimes you have to strike repeatedly in rapid succession to get a spray of sparks. Striking the flint and steel together to get sparks is the first skill to master in this fire-making process. If you don't really need a fire, it's fun to do all by itself, especially in the dark.

PRACTICE CATCHING SPARKS
Once you get a spark, you need a way for it to become an ember. Once you get an ember, you need to put it into dry tinder and blow it into a flame.

TURN A SPARK TO AN EMBER ON BURNT CLOTH OR STEEL WOOL
Catch the spark on a material that will allow it to become an ember. Mountain folk and pioneers used charred remnants of cloth to catch the sparks they made striking flint and steel together. I often use super-fine steel wool. A spark lands in the burnt cloth or steel wool, spreads out into the steel strands, and becomes a good-size glowing ember. This ember is then put into the tinder bundle, just as you did with the little pile of wood-dust embers from your hand-drill fire making (see Make a Matchless Campfire, p. 165).

Burnt cloth made from natural fibers is the kind that catches sparks. Old jeans or canvas pants, as well as pieces of tightly woven linen or hemp cloth, can be used. You want to burn the cloth all the way through so that it's a dark black color, but you don't want to burn it so much that it falls apart.

You're going to take a little section of the cloth and hold it with the flint chip, pressing the two together as you strike sparks with the metal. If you haven't burned the cloth well enough, the sparks that land on it won't grow, spread out, and create an ember. If you use super-fine steel wool, it gets held with the flint chip just like the charred cloth would.

♠♠ MAKE BURNT OR CHARRED CLOTH

Cut strips of cloth about 1 foot long and 1 inch wide, and roll them up like a cloth bandage. Place these little rolls of fabric in a small, thin-walled metal container, similar to the ones Altoids come in.

Next time you have a campfire, place the whole container in the coals. The container will burn and discolor, and the cloth inside will char. You're going to have to play around a little bit with this. If you leave it in too long, the cloth will disintegrate. If you don't leave it in long enough, you'll have unburned places throughout the cloth, and it won't catch sparks well or allow the sparks to turn into embers.

It's a little ironic that you have to have a fire in the first place to make the burnt cloth needed to make a flint and steel fire.

♠♠ PRACTICE TURNING SPARKS TO EMBERS

After you've had a lot of practice striking sparks, practice striking sparks that land on the burnt cloth and spread out into an ember. In general, if you have a good sparking metal without too much or too little carbon content, sparks fly out and downward at an angle, like the sparks you see when you hold a piece of metal to an electric grinder if the wheel is rotating toward you. On the other hand, sparks can go out in all kinds of random directions, so I like to tuck a little piece of the charred cloth under my thumb and under my pointer finger when I'm holding the flint chip. This gives my sparks a landing pad above and below the edge of the flint. If I'm depending on that fire, I like to hedge my bets!

PUT THE EMBER IN THE TINDER BUNDLE

I'm guessing you've already practiced blowing the tinder bundle into a flame. If so, all you have to do now to make a flint and steel fire is put all these parts you've practiced together.

GATHER WILD FOOD IN THE FOREST

Now that you are entertaining the idea of harvesting free, healthful wild food in urban, suburban, and rural areas, you are probably already wondering what foods are available when you go wandering through the woods. So many foods are available to the wild harvester.

KNOWLEDGE

I mentioned several of my favorite books for learning to identify wild food and medicine in Gather Wild Food in the City, p. 57. Hopefully you have found them very useful in the urban and suburban areas.

Whatever it is you haven't found yet, in and around the homestead or in the parking lots of the shopping centers, is out there waiting for you in the woods. Take a good plant guide with you every time you go. It won't take long before you greet the plants on a first-name basis and know exactly where to look when you have a particular recipe in mind.

MAKE FLOUR FROM ACORNS

Acorns are one of my favorite things to collect in the fall. I love acorn muffins and pancakes, acorn cranberry bread, and acorn stuffing. **White oak acorns** can usually be harvested, ground down into flour, and added into any recipe you choose, without any other

preparation. Many other acorn varieties have a high amount of tannic acid, making them taste bitter.

At Earth Knack we grind the acorns with a mano and metate, but at home you can use a high-powered blender or a small home-size grinding wheel.

LEACHING TANNINS OUT OF ACORN MEATS

Red, black, and **scrub acorn** varieties can be ground down into coarse meal or flour and then covered in fresh water, which pulls out the tannic acid. The water will turn dark golden brown. Drain and cover the flour with water repeatedly until the water no longer has a color in it. Then you can dry the flour out and add it to any recipe you want.

To dry the flour, spread a thin layer of the meal on a baking sheet and set it in the sun for several hours, or put it in a gas oven with the pilot light running, or a food dehydrator overnight. If you're going to cook right away, add the wet flour into the recipe.

STORING THE GROUND ACORN MEAL

It's not always easy to dry the flour out; instead, you can take little handfuls of the wet flour and throw it in a plastic bag to freeze. If you know exactly how much you want in the recipes you are using, you can freeze it in those amounts.

KNOWLEDGE

Tannic acid is found in the bark of hardwood trees, in many nuts, shells, and husks, and in a variety of plants and woods. Back in the day, people who wanted to soften hides to make leather made big vats of tannic acid by soaking bark in water for a long period of time. The hides were then soaked in this acidic water, and the acid broke down the glue molecules in the hide.

Elmer's glue and other wood glues are made by cooking down hides, hooves, and other animal parts. When we want rawhide for a drum or rattle, it is the glue in the hide that allows it to hold stiff. When we want buckskin—soft, supple clothing leather—we eliminate the glue. Tannic acid is one of the things that can eliminate the glue in a hide, and it is also the thing that makes the acorn bitter.

STUDY AND LEARN TO IDENTIFY EDIBLE MUSHROOMS

It has taken me most of my life to begin enjoying mushrooms. As a child, I found them slippery and slimy, and eating them felt like swallowing leeches. However, my interest in wild edibles and plants in general has kept me in the company of mushrooms. Everywhere I go, there they are. I've always been fascinated by how they grow, look, reproduce—and I just love the word spore! But eat them? No way!

Jerry LaValle is a mycologist (a fancy name for a mushroom know-it-all). His enthusiasm for oyster mushrooms convinced me to give them a try one day. Maybe it was the butter, but eating those mushrooms added a whole new dimension to my gastronomic experience.

There are only a few mushrooms that I really like, but they are absolutely delicious, and I would encourage anyone to learn more about mushrooms. Pick one or two that you really like and learn to use them in healthy, happy ways. Look to the books to start you on your mushroom search. David Arora's

All That the Rain Promises and More. . . is my favorite mushroom book. The title alone could make you feel kindly toward mushrooms!

As with any wild plant that you are not familiar with, don't assume it is edible just because it looks good or smells good. Never pop anything into your mouth, or even take a very tiny nibble, unless you are certain it is something you can safely eat.

HUNTING, TRAPPING, SNARING

Besides tree nuts, mushrooms, and plants, the woods are full of small game. In fact, I make a point to put a tureen of squirrel gravy on the Thanksgiving table every year. Squirrels and other game can be snared, trapped, or hunted using some of the weaponry we've talked about in this book. (See Throwing Sticks and Boomerangs, p. 11, and Spear and Hoop Game, p. 103.) In *Wildwood Wisdom*, a book on wilderness living from the 1940s by Ellsworth Jaeger, there is a diagram for a very effective twitch-up snare. Laws about hunting, trapping, or snaring vary from area to area, so if you're interested in procuring meat for the table in this way, make sure you know all the regulations.

A HUNTING ETHIC

I hunt meat because I want to take personal responsibility for the life I take to sustain my own. Hunting is not an easy activity for me, but I've been going these last thirty years, and crying every time I kill something, because I'm committed to being part of the process. I'm committed to taking that responsibility. I'm not afraid to feel deeply and openly my gratitude for being alive each day on this planet. I'm grateful to know how to hunt and that my children have grown up hunting.

TRULY HEALTHY NOURISHMENT

We have been able to provide ourselves with some of the healthiest food we eat because we hunt. The animals that roam the area where we live breathe some of the cleanest air, drink some of the cleanest water, and forage across open land full of nourishing wild plant life. They eat the plants and each other, and the meat that they become is just plain good. I could go buy a whole bag of organic vegetables grown somewhere in central California, and they wouldn't come close to being as clean as the meat I hunt here at home.

▲▲▲ MAKING JERKY

If you decide hunting is for you and you spend a bit of time out in the woods hunting, snaring, or trapping, you're going to need a way to preserve the meat well, quickly, and safely. Making jerky is a great way to do all three of these things. You can make jerky with any meat.

If you're making the jerky out in the woods, there are a few things you need to consider.

QUESTIONS

What kind of critters are around who are going to want to come into your camp if you lay out a bunch of raw meat? How are you going to keep the flies off the meat? Are you going to be able to get the jerky cured, or dried well, in enough time before rain comes?

KNOWLEDGE
KEEPING FLIES OFF

You need to slice the meat thinly because flies won't lay eggs in any medium that doesn't have enough moisture. Fly eggs need a certain amount of moisture to hatch. Before laying their eggs on something, they determine the amount of moisture. When you cut the meat very thin, a fly rejects the meat as a good egg-laying area. Sometimes I wonder why we think we're the ones who are so smart.

SLICE THE MEAT WITH THE GRAIN

Cut the meat down the length of the grain. The pieces will hold together better if the long, fibrous muscle tissue runs down the whole piece. When you're cooking a stew, you want to cut across the grain, allowing the little chunks of meat to become more tender and easier to chew. You'll also want to cut across the grain if you're planning to grind your meat, especially if you have a hand grinder or a small, lightweight home grinder. But for jerky, go along the grain line, not against it.

IDEA
ACCORDION SLICE THE MEAT

You can make one big sheet of meat instead of strips. Start on one side of the muscle and make a thin cut downward with the grain. Just before you cut through, flip the whole muscle over and, moving just about $1/8$ inch from where you cut the first time, slice all the way back down through the muscle the other way. Repeat this flipping and slicing procedure all the way across the muscle. Grip the two outer cuts, and you can pull the whole muscle out like an accordion. It will be in one big sheet of meat. This can be a lot easier to handle than a lot of little strips of meat. If it starts to rain, it's easier to run under cover with it as well.

DRY THE MEAT

Make a tripod of sticks and put them on the leeward edge of your fire pit. Wrap some string or lashing around the tripod, spiraling downward. Make sure the string is taut and secure. Hang the meat from the string.

Make a smoky fire and let the breeze blow the smoke over the curing meat. This will keep bugs away from the meat. If you let enough smoke blow over and around the meat, it may have a slightly smoky flavor, but what you are doing here is simply drying the meat and letting the smoke blow over it to keep bugs away.

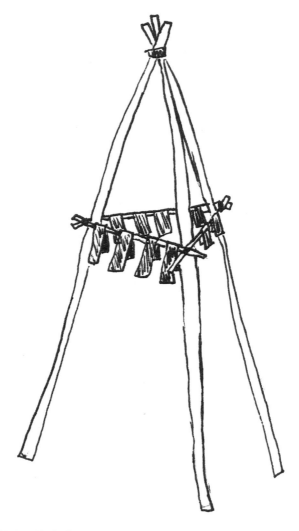

KNOWLEDGE

Where there is smoke, is there fire? Animals think so! It helps keep other critters away from your camp. Wild animals do not like smoke. Smoke means fire; fire means run. You can see this principle in action when a beekeeper uses a smoker to work with a hive. In the case of the bees, they go in and start grabbing up all their honey so that they can run away from the forest fire with some food stores to start over again somewhere else. While the bees are busy gorging on honey, the beekeeper has a little bit of time to do whatever hive maintenance is needed. By the time the maintenance is over and the smoke has cleared, the bees decide there probably isn't a forest fire after all and go back to their regular business. If animals are truly wild, they have an instinct to run from smoke. On the other hand, if animals are truly hungry, the smell of meat is very attractive.

FLAVORING THE JERKY

There are lots of great jerky recipes with all kinds of marinating sauces and spices. A lot of these recipes include ingredients that help tenderize and soften the meat. Using salt on your meat strips helps preserve the meat and also helps keep pests away. I simply rub salt and pepper on the meat strips before I hang them and call it good.

STORING THE JERKY

Once the meat is dry, you can keep it indefinitely in a glass jar with a lid or in a sealed bag. You can use one of those fancy vacuum sealer machines, or you can make your jerky last even longer by storing it in a refrigerator or the freezer. In my mind, the cool part of making jerky is being able to preserve meat in a way that does not require modern systems. However you decide to keep it, keeping it dry is important.

DUTCH OVEN COOKING

Dutch oven cooking is an old-timey pioneer style of cooking on a fire. A Dutch oven is a heavy, round, thick-walled cast iron pot. It usually has legs and a flat lid. The legs keep the pot up and out of the ashes and allow you to add or subtract coals from underneath the pot, adjusting the temperature as necessary. The legs also keep the pot from crushing the coals, which robs them of oxygen, reducing the burn and diminishing heat. The flat lid supports a layer of coals, so the pot is also being heated from the top. The coals on top and on bottom create an oven effect.

Due to its weight and size, this is not a backpacking pot. It is great for car camping or canoe trips, big group campsites with established fire pits, and also works wonderfully in the backyard, out on the front porch, or even out on the neighborhood sidewalk if any of these areas offer a safe way to make a fire. Dutch oven cooking can be a bit of a production, but it is a lot of fun.

DEDICATED TOOLS

You'll want to have two tools in addition to your fire poker: a round-point metal shovel with a full-length handle and a rock rake. Paint some red stripes or some other kind of design on the handles so you know that they are dedicated fire tools. You don't want to use just any tools, especially ones you care about, when you are tending the fire. The heat of the fire changes the quality of metal tools. After they've been used many times in the fire, they lose their original hardness, or temper, and are no longer good tools for the jobs that they were made to do.

USE LIKE A REGULAR OVEN

Pretty much anything you can cook in a regular home oven, you can cook in a Dutch oven with coals from the fire pit. Try regular recipes you use in the kitchen oven.

TIP

One of the tricks to cooking on the fire is getting the fire started early enough to build up heat and make enough hot coals to work with to maintain cooking temperatures. Some coals burn up quickly while others last a longer time. Some wood burns to ash very rapidly, forming very little coal that is good for cooking. Some coals burn at a lower temperature than others. Over time, you will become familiar with all these variations.

BRIQUETTES OR COALS

Because natural resources are unpredictable, some Dutch oven cooks have created recipes with directions that instruct you to use charcoal briquettes instead of coals. Briquettes are uniform and burn evenly, give a consistent heat, and last about the same amount of time as coals. If you find a Dutch oven recipe book, it will probably be full of this information.

I would rather take my chances with coals. I like working with natural materials and resources. I do what I do and live the way I live to relate with and experience nature more fully. I am always looking to distill a knowing or doing down to its essence. There is nothing in this book that couldn't be made more complicated or be done with manufactured materials. In fact, modern life, in the effort to make things easier and more convenient, has created a very complicated paradigm.

IDEA

In Light a One-Match Campfire, p. 151, we mentioned recycling charcoal. Save chunks of charcoal from past fires to use for making your own briquettes. They heat up in the next fire more quickly, and you don't have to wait for the entire log to burn down, so you can start cooking sooner. This can be convenient, like store-bought briquettes, and that's nice. The difference is that you are a part of the process. Being present and participating affords great satisfaction to the willing. Making briquettes might seem like a simple example, but it is a start.

IMAGINE

You wander through the woods, enveloped in nature, gathering firewood. You create the fire with two of the sticks that you find in the woods. You tend the fire and wait for the right cooking coals. Much of the food in the Dutch oven you harvested in the wild. You are not just having a meal, but you are deeply, intimately, fully connected to each part of the process. As you eat, you remember the hunt, the gather, the time in nature. You are not just getting the nutrition of the food; you're getting the full nutrition of the experience. This is good stuff. This is being a part of the process. This takes time. And taking time writes a different story than choosing convenience.

ROAST A WHOLE BIRD

1 whole bird of choice (store bought or wild harvested) that will fit into your Dutch oven

Salt and pepper, to taste

Potatoes, cut into chunks

Carrots, cut into chunks

Apples, cut into chunks

Onions, cut into chunks

Olive oil, to coat the vegetables

Lemon pepper, to taste

Wild greens, to taste

Water, as needed

Rub the poultry with salt and pepper. Toss the potatoes, carrots, apples, and onions in the olive oil and lemon pepper. Place a layer of the vegetables on the bottom of a Dutch oven, set the bird on top, add in the rest of the vegetables, sprinkle the wild greens all over the top, add several cups of water or wild greens infusion (see Wild Medicinal Plants and Tea Infusions, p. 83), and put on the cover.

PREPARE THE COALS

Rake out a little round pad of coals slightly larger than the Dutch oven itself, and gently flatten it down. Set the Dutch oven on the coals and put two shovelfuls of coals on the flat lid. Make sure not to put a pile of ash on the lid. Get the hot coals right against the metal of the pot. Use the bottom of the shovel to flatten the coals on the lid so that there is a consistent thickness of coals all around the lid. Now you can relax and let it cook for a while. Don't worry about it. If you keep lifting the lid to check it, it will never cook.

KEEP THE ASH OUT

Carefully lift the lid, keeping it level so that no coal or ash falls into the food, and set it on the rocks around the fire or a grilling grate elevated out of the ash. If you set the lid down in the ash or the dirt, that dirt or ash will fall in when you go to put the lid back on the food.

ADJUSTING TEMPERATURE

If you find that the food on the bottom is well-done but the top is not, put the lid back on with some fresh coals and set the Dutch oven to the side of the fire pit area with no coals underneath. If the food on top is well done and the bottom is not, make a new bed of coals for the bottom and don't add any more to the top.

GENERAL COOKING METHOD

Regardless of what recipe you make, the cooking method is pretty much the same. You might add more coals to the top and bottom of the oven for something that needs to get much hotter, or you will use fewer coals if it needs to cook on a low temperature. When you think it's done, check it. Use what you know about baking in the kitchen to make this guesstimate. If you can smell the cooked food and the scent makes you hungry, chances are your food is ready. One of the great things about roasting in the Dutch oven is the way it seals in the juices. The roasted meals are much more moist than when cooked in a conventional oven.

MAKE A COBBLER

Cobblers are really fun to make in a Dutch oven. My friend Ken Wee makes the best Dutch oven cobblers! He'll get a whole row of Dutch ovens going all at once to cook cobbler for a big camp.

FILLING

Enough fruit to fill your oven, cut into slices or chunks—peaches, apples, and blueberries work well

Cinnamon, ginger, and nutmeg, to taste

Sugar, to taste

3 heaping tablespoons tapioca

1/4 cup lemon juice

1/2 stick butter, grated

1/2 cup apple juice

➡

BATTER

Flour (about 3 cups) to make a
* 2-inch-thick batter across the top*
* layer of your Dutch oven*
3 heaping teaspoons baking powder
1/4 teaspoon baking soda
1 teaspoons salt
2 tablespoons sugar
Cinnamon and ginger, to taste
Water to make a sticky biscuit-like
* dough*

TOPPING

1/2 cup brown sugar
1/4 cup sugar
2 tablespoons flour
Pinch of cinnamon
1/2 stick butter

Before you begin preparing the cobbler, prepare the coals as discussed in the previous recipe.

Sprinkle the fruit with cinnamon, ginger, nutmeg, sugar, tapioca, butter, and apple juice. Stir it all together and let the mixture sit for about 1 hour to pull the juices out of the fruit.

While the fruit is sitting, begin preparing the batter. Mix together the flour, baking powder, baking soda, salt, sugar, cinnamon, and ginger.

Set aside. Do not add the water.

In a small bowl, combine the brown sugar, granulated sugar, flour, and cinnamon. Mix it all up and grate the butter over the top. Mash it all together with a fork, turning the mixture into a crumbly topping. You will sprinkle this on top of the cake batter before you put the lid on the Dutch oven.

When the juices have started to flow from the fruit chunks, stir the filling and pour it into the bottom of the Dutch oven. Add the water to the dry dough mixture, and stir just until everything is wet. Pour the batter over the fruit in an even layer about 2 inches thick.

Sprinkle the crumbly topping mix over the batter. Put the lid on the oven, place the oven on the coals, and add coals to the lid. You should keep an eye on the cobbler. Between the sugar and butter, it's easy to burn this dessert. Let the cobbler cook until the juices are bubbling up from underneath the cobbler topping and the crust is golden brown. You will never need to make another s'more again!

OTHER RECIPE IDEAS

Pizza, cinnamon rolls, quiche, and lasagna all come out wonderfully in the Dutch oven. Breakfast casseroles can be made with egg, grated cheese, sausage, bacon, broccoli, or whatever else you like. Cut the sausage, bacon, and broccoli into small pieces and grate some cheese. Whip up a bunch of eggs with cream, and stir in salt, pepper, dill, the chopped meat and broccoli, and the grated cheese. Pour the mixture it into your Dutch oven. It will puff up like a soufflé, and you can cut into the middle to see if it is solid all the way through before you take it off the coals. While it's cooking, chop up a bunch of fresh tomatoes and sprinkle them with lemon pepper and a few shakes of balsamic vinegar. Spoon some of this mixture over the hot slices of breakfast casserole on each plate.

SKEWER FOODS

Shish kebabs are also a bunch of fun, and after the cutting up of everything, it's a pretty simple way to cook food. Get that coal bed ready, set up two forked sticks or a little tripod on either side of the ooal bed. Cut up all the foods you love to grill, and then skewer them on a long metal rod. Set each end of the rod into the forked sticks or tripod, about 8 to 10 inches over the coals. Rotate the skewer periodically until everything is cooked. That's pretty simple!

You can also use individual skewers, or even carved wooden sticks like you would use to roast marshmallows, and everyone can roast their own food several chunks at a time. Sausages are fun for everyone to cook on their own. You can also wrap a coil of bread dough around the stick and slowly rotate it until the bread puffs up and browns! It's pretty entertaining. Try this with the ash cake dough that you made (see Make Meals on the Campfire Coals, p. 201).

MAKE WILLOW OR GRASS BASKETS

We all need a way to carry our stuff. Perhaps this activity will inspire you to make your carry-along bag (see Survival Shelters, p. 183) into a carry-along basket instead!

HISTORY

The skill of twining a basket is very old, and evidence of this knowledge is found on all continents. In fact, whole-shoot twining techniques, where the whole willow shoots are the weaving material, are a pandemic ancestral skill. By pandemic I mean that we can find evidence that all of our ancestors on all continents practiced the same skill. This idea always gives me delicious tingles.

CONSIDER

With all the fuss and struggle and meanness in the modern world centering on religion, politics, and race, I think it's perfectly wonderful to remember that we all share a heritage in the ancestral skills. We are twined together through the long epochs of history by a shared knowing, by a shared doing. How much happier it is to concentrate on the things that bind us—or should I say the things that twine us—together.

I am going to describe how to twine a basket using whole shoots of **willow**. You could use this same technique with grass for a more supple, tightly spaced basket, or with bark fibers, string, rope, or buckskin lacing for a very flexible bag-like basket. Split spruce roots actually make a watertight basket; when you put the water inside, it swells the roots and seals the gaps. How cool is that?! (See Resources, p. 302, for more information on spruce basket weaving.)

MAKE A WILLOW BASKET

GATHER MATERIALS

First, you need to go out and collect your willow shoots. Straight, supple willows can be found lining ditches and along roadsides where water stands. Lake shores and riverbanks are another place to look for willow shoots. The shoots along roadways are really good for baskets because the county maintenance departments come and mow the edges of the roads, which encourages the willow to send up straight, young shoots that are perfect for basket making.

KEEP WILLOWS DAMP

Collect more willows than you think you will need. Keep all the cut ends bundled together. When you get to the place that you're going to sit and weave the basket, place all the cut ends in water. This will help keep the willows flexible and moist. If you're not in a place where there is water, cover the whole bundle with a damp towel, and keep it in the shade while you work.

CHOOSE YOUR SHOOTS

Pick an uneven number of willow shoots to begin. Select shoots from your bundle that are about the same length and width. Let's just pick thirty-three for starters. Put all the cut ends together, hold them in your hands, and tap them gently on the ground so that the ends are equal with each other.

TIE TIPS IN A KNOT

Run your hands up the willows. Grab the whole bundle near the tips (do not try to make the tips even) and twist them together, tying them in an overhand knot. Make sure all the ends are caught into the knot, and then pull it nice and tight.

Make yourself a quick piece of string from some plant fiber, long enough to tie a tight knot just above and just below the knot you made in the willows. You can cut the string to tie these two places or leave it long. This is a little insurance as you get started.

LOTS OF METHODS

This is a simple, easy start. There are lots of ways to make a basket. There are lots of ways to start a basket. Once you get good at the

➡

twining technique and shaping the basket, you can look into all different kinds of starting techniques.

WEAVER SHOOTS

Hold the knot in your lap with the loose ends pointed away from you. Reach close to the knot and pull up two willows that are right next to each other. These two willows are going to be your weavers. This means they will weave around and around the basket. These are the two you will start twining or twisting.

SPOKE SHOOTS

The rest of the willows are going to be your spokes, like the spokes on a wheel. These spokes will form the framework of the basket. You get to create the shape of the basket by bending these willows at more or less of an angle out, up, or in. You

shape the spoke the way you want it, and then you twine the weavers together, trapping the spoke in between them to hold it in place.

STAY THE COURSE

When you first start, you're not going to feel like you're in control of shaping the basket at all. Just keep going. Over time, you become proficient at twining, spacing, and shaping and the basket forms according to your vision.

BEGIN THE TWINING TECHNIQUE

Holding the first two willows that are going to be your weavers, you'll take the closest willow next to the weavers and push it in between the two of them. The weavers are going out to the side horizontally, and the spoke is sticking straight up. When you've got

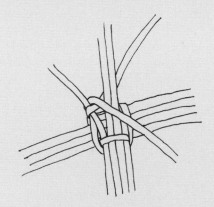
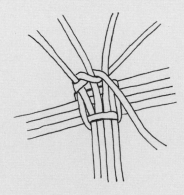

the spoke pushed snug up against the two weavers, grip the weavers between your thumb and pointer finger and give them a twist away from you. Just turn them together between your thumb and finger, so the weaver that was in front is now to the back and over the other weaver.

It's like you just made a little X and the spoke is trapped in the half of the X that is closest to where the weavers started. Now, stick a second spoke right into the half of the X that is still open, and snug it up close. Twist the weavers again. Always twist them away from you. Continue snugging in the spokes and twisting the weavers until you have gone all the way around and every spoke is trapped between the weavers in an orderly little circle. You have just accomplished one row of twining.

SUPPORT SPOKES IN YOUR LAP

Remember to always twist, or twine, the same way. I twine away from me because I find it easier to control the shape of the spokes. As the basket forms, and I con- tinue to go around row after row, I use my lap as a support. Twisting

away with the weavers, I get to put a little downward pressure on the spoke and push against my legs to help hold the spoke right where I want it to be.

START THE SECOND ROW OF TWINING

When you've gotten around to where you started on that first circle, just jump up a little on the first spoke you started with and go right back around again. The twining will have a slight spiral moving upward. Keep in mind that these weavers aren't infinitely long, so as you come to the thicker end of each weaver, place the thin end of a new one parallel with the old one, with the ends overlapping several inches. Hold it in place and continue twining it as if it is the same weaver.

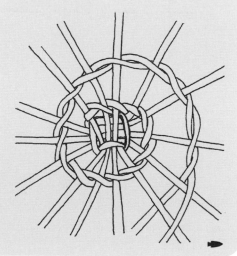

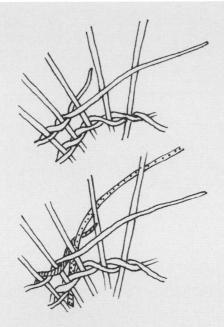

with the top of the spoke. One side of the staple runs all the way back down to the knot. The top of the staple runs right along the top edge of twining and becomes your finished top edge, and the second, short side of the staple runs down along the side of the next spoke and stays secure there.

You want to make these little corner bends so they fit neatly along the top rim of the last twining row. You have to push pretty hard to get the short end down into the twists that are holding the other spoke, but that tightness is what helps it hold in place.

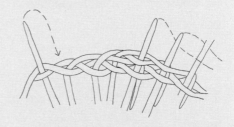

SPLICING TECHNIQUE

This is going to feel a little awkward and fumbly at first, but you will get used to it. Adding weavers in is called splicing. There are a lot of splicing methods, and some of them really lock the ends down tight as you work. I'm trying to get you started here in the simplest way possible. After you get the technique, you can try all kinds of variations.

USE YOUR BONE AWL

You can help apply pressure to places in the basket that are tight and need adjusting, or open up the twists to help push the spoke end through to finish the top rim, by using a bone awl (see Make a Bone Knife or Awl, p. 209).

FINISHING THE TOP EDGE

You want to weave up and around the spokes, stopping when the top length of your spokes is still long enough to bend into the spokes next to them. It's like you're making a little square-cornered staple

USES FOR BONE AWL

If you have a spoke that breaks off while you're working, a bone awl can help open up the twists while you shove a new spoke in place next to the broken one. If you have spliced in a weaver and it just won't stay in place, you can use the bone awl to open up a few twists holding a nearby spoke. Shove the tip of the new weaver down through the opened twists along that spoke, letting the twists close up around the tip as you remove the awl. This will hold the weaver end securely as you continue to twine. If you are making this basket out of grasses or other softer materials, the bone awl is going to be very helpful.

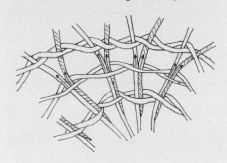

When you've got all the spoke ends pushed down into their neighboring spoke, the basket body is finished. My friend Jerry calls this activity willow wrestling. However, he makes some of the most intricate and lovely baskets I have seen, and I am proud to have been his teacher, even if my baskets still look like I wrestle willows!

MAKE A WOOD BURN BOWL

One way you can use fire as a tool is to make containers from wood using a hollow blow tube to keep a coal burning down into the wood and burning out the interior space. An easy project to start with is making a wooden bowl. First you make the blow tube, then you make the fire.

KNOWLEDGE

The hollow blow tube, another ancestral tool, is easy to make and serves a variety of purposes. This blow tube is a hollow reed that concentrates the air you blow into it in one direction. This makes a very forceful delivery of something from the tube, like air helping to ignite reluctant tinder by increasing the oxygen or a dart for hunting.

BLOW DARTS

A traditional hunting weapon of the Cherokee was comprised of a very small dart with spiral-wrapped thistle down as fletching. This dart was tucked into the top of a hollowed length of **river cane**, a bamboo-like plant indigenous to the southeast. Evidence of ancestral blowgun and dart weapons technology can be found on all continents.

SPRAY GUNS

Another great use for a blow tube is spraying pigment paints onto a surface you want to decorate. The concentrated force allows you to cover a large area with a single blowing. It's the original spray gun, and it was used worldwide (another pandemic technology) to make hand outline pictographs.

FIRE TOOL

A blow tube is a great thing for the fire tender to keep near the fire pit. In making wooden bowls or other containers, a blow tube increases the coal heat to aid continual, controlled burning. This allows you to make a very small, deep hole in a chunk of log.

▲▲ MAKE A BLOW TUBE TOOL

GATHER MATERIALS

River cane, **reed grass** (western states), and many other segmented, hollow-stemmed plants can be found for making blow tubes. You can also hollow out the pithy-centered plants like **mullein** or **horseweed,** but this might be more work than finding a hollow-stemmed plant.

CLEAR THE TUBE

You are going to remove one hollow section of a segmented plant to make a blow tube. At each node between segments, there is a little wall of softer plant material. You will gently score around the top and bottom of the segment or section and work your sharp edge round and round until you score through to the hollow center. You don't want to snap it off because the whole hollow section will crack,

and then the air won't concentrate in the direction you're blowing it.

PITCH ANY CRACKS

If you're in the middle of a project and your blow tube gets a crack, you can make up some pitch glue (see How to Make a Drum, p. 89). Smear the pitch glue up and down the crack in the tube to prevent the air from leaking out.

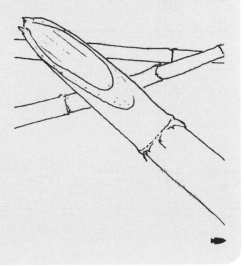

NOTE

Pitch heats up quickly, and if you use it as a blow tube patch, you could burn your fingers. The tube gets hot, especially if it is short. Keep in mind that pitch also melts with heat, so you might have to reapply it often. Making several blow tubes right away is a good idea; not only will you have spares, but you'll also use the whole plant and avoid wasting any of the harvest.

BEVEL THE TOP EDGE

Once you have the hollow segment removed from the main part of the plant, you can gently bevel the edge that you will blow into so that it's a little bit easier on your lips. However, if your lips feel a little chapped after using the blow tube, use a bit of that wonderful salve you made (see Make Healing Salves, p. 227).

MAKE A LONG TUBE AS A FIRE-TENDING TOOL

You could also use the whole plant to make a longer blow tube. It would mean you could blow the fire up without stooping over. The Cherokee used a long tube for their blow darts, offering better aim.

MAKE A BORING ROD

To make a longer blow tube from one plant, you need to find a firm piece of stick and carve it thin enough to fit inside the segmented plant without breaking. Gently push the stick back and forth to break through the little walls at each node that separate the segments, using it like a boring rod. The stick would need to be long enough to hold onto and press up through half the length you want the final blow tube to be. Turn the blow tube around and run the stick through other side. If you're going to go through all that trouble to carve the stick thin enough to fit into the hollow stem, you might as well not make the stick any longer than you have to.

♠♠ MAKE A WOODEN BURN BOWL

Saw an 8- or 9-inch-long section from a log that also has an 8- or 9-inch diameter. Take a sharp stone wedge and set it right at the center of one of the cut ends. You could also use your Old Hickory knife. Either way, take a heavy

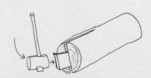

stone and knock the sharp edge down through the log, splitting it equally in half.

SET THE COAL ON THE WOOD

Pick out a coal from the fire that is 1 or 2 inches long, and place it right in the center of the log split. Let the coal sit for a moment and make a charred spot on the wood.

BLOW TUBE USE

Using a hollow blow tube, gently blow at the base of the small coal, using a stick to hold the coal in place from the top so that it won't blow away. As you blow, the heat from the coal will move into the charred wood and begin to turn the charred spot into a coal of its own.

BLOW AIR

CONTINUALLY REMOVE THE TOP LAYER OF CHAR

Allow the burn to sink down and out to form the interior shape of a bowl within the split log. Throughout the process, periodically use the sharp edge of your stone tool to scrape away the charcoal dust and knock it back

into the fire. The most burnt layer of wood actually prevents efficient burning. When one coal diminishes and loses its heat, toss it back in the fire and pick out a fresh one.

Make sure to keep your back to the breeze and let the smoke blow away from you.

FINISH THE BOWL SHAPE

Once you've finished making the interior of the bowl as large as you want, scrape out all the char and smooth the inside by rubbing it with sand, sandpaper, or a rough, round sandstone-type rock. The smoother the inside of the bowl is, the easier it will be to clean. Round off the outer edges of the log half, smoothing and shaping them. Finally, take some fat or oil and rub it into the wood. Take a little piece of leather or a rag, and rub the inside of the bowl hard and vigorously to get the fat to penetrate the wood.

DECORATE THE BOWL

You can draw or carve your name or any design you want into the outer edge of the bowl.

CONCLUSION

I trust the ideas and skills presented here will get you out in the healthy open air and foster new perspectives on confidence, options, and a bigger sense of our place in history. More than that, if you have young ones in your community, I hope you will get excited and involved with the activities and learning, and be inspired to mentor others. "Do as I say," has never really worked. Children are masters of imitation. If we are enthusiastically going about doing these healthy, happy things, they will be right there beside us, growing and learning in a healthy, happy way.

There are so many things we do in modern life that are really ancestral skills dressed up in modern clothes! As you incorporate more outdoor living skills, it will be fun to draw your own conclusions about the path of cultural, societal, and daily living skills evolution.

Money is one of those things that is just dressed up differently these days. Back in the day, food and resources were traded from place to place. As people moved from subsistence living to acquiring possessions and forming large societies, different items held value at different times to purchase trifles, trinkets, practicalities, dreams, and even kingdoms. In many places, and in many cultures through a long part of history, shells served as the money and status of the times.

I've collected a lot of shells over the years, and unlike most people, I'm always using them. I use them to hold fat for lamps, to hold pigment paints, to shape and smooth clay (as well as grind them into a powder to mix with the clay I use), to scrape animal hides, for cutters (shells actually make fairly good knives), and I use shards of shell to scrape bow staves. What I haven't ever used them for is money.

Sometimes I imagine if I lived a long time ago, how very wealthy I would be with all my piles of shells. I don't spend too much time imagining that though, because I am one of the richest women I know! I hope that as you take more time in nature and learn these skills, incorporating them into your life and sharing them with your friends and family, you will feel as rich as I do.

LIST OF PLANTS

BASSWOOOD/LINDEN

CATTAIL

CLOVER

RESOURCES

BOOKS

WILD FOOD AND MEDICINE

Arora, David. *All That the Rain Promises and More: A Hip Pocket Guide to Western Mushrooms*. Berkley: Ten Speed Press, 1991.

Blankenship, Bart, and Robin Blankenship. *Earth Knack: Stone Age Skills for the 21st Century*. Layton, UT: Gibbs Smith, Publisher, 1996.

Elliott, Douglas B. *Wild Roots: A Forager's Guide to the Edible and Medicinal Roots, Tubers, Corms, and Rhizomes of North America*. Rochester, VT: Healing Arts Press, 1995

Gladstar, Rosemary. *Rosemary Gladstar's Family Herbal: A Guide to Living Life with Energy, Health, and Vitality*. North Adams, MA: Storey Books, 2001.

Harris, Ben Charles. *Eat the Weeds*. Barre, MA: Barre Publishers, 1968.

Jaeger, Ellsworth. *Wildwood Wisdom*. Bolinas, CA: Shelter Publications, 1992.

Seebeck, Cattail Bob. *Survival Plants of Colorado*. Drake, CO: Cattail Publishing, 2012.

Thayer, Samuel. *The Forager's Harvest: A Guide to Identifying, Harvesting, and Preparing Edible Wild Plants*. Ogema, WI: Forager's Harvest Press, 2006.

Weed, Susun S. *Wise Woman Herbal for the Childbearing Year*. Woodstock, NY: Ash Tree Publishing, 1985.

SURVIVAL/PRIMITIVE SKILLS

Blankenship, Bart, and Robin Blankenship. *Earth Knack: Stone Age Skills for the 21st Century*. Layton, UT: Gibbs Smith, Publisher, 1996.

MacPherson, John, and Geri MacPherson. *Naked Into The Wilderness: Primitive Wilderness Living and Survival Skills*. Randolph, KS: Prairie Wolf Press, 1993.

PRIMITIVE SKILLS EDUCATIONAL EVENTS

The Bulletin of Primitive Technology. Editor: Dave Wescott. Issue: Spring 2015: No. 49. ISSN 1078-4845.

KNOWLEDGE/OUTDOOR INTEREST

Bliss, Anne. *North American Dye Plants*. Loveland, CO: Interweave Press, 1993.

Eaton, S. Boyd, Marjorie Shostak, and Melvin Konner. *The Paleolithic Prescription: A Program of Diet and Exercise and a Design for Living*. New York: Harper & Row, 1988.

Echols, Ray. *A Thru-Hiker's Heart: Tales of the Pacific Crest Trail*. Mariposa, CA: Tuolumne Press, 2009.

Halacy, Beth, and Dan Halacy. *Cooking With The Sun*. Lafayette, CA: Morning Sun Press, 1978.

Mionczynski, John. *The Pack Goat*. Boulder, CO: Pruett Publishing, 1992.

Patten, Bob. *Old Tools—New Eyes: A Primal Primer of Flintknapping*. Denver: Stone Dagger Publications, 1999.

Paul, Frances. *Spruce Root Basketry of the Alaska Tlingit*. Lawrence, KS: Department of the Interior, Bureau of Indian Affairs, 1944.

Rey, H.A. *Find the Constellations*. Boston: Houghton Mifflin Harcourt, 2008.

———. *The Stars: A New Way to See Them*. Boston: Houghton Mifflin Harcourt, 2008.

Sloane, Eric. *A Reverence for Wood*. New York: Ballantine Books, 1965.

Wilkinson, Ernest. *Snow Caves for Fun and Survival*. Boulder, CO: Johnson Printing, 1992.

PLACES

Cahokia Mounds State Historic Site.
Collinsville, Illinois.

Chaco Culture National Historical Park.
Nageezi, New Mexico.

SONGS AND STORIES

Billy Jonas Band. *Build It Back Again*. Bang-A-Bucket
Music. 2014, compact disc.

Blankenship, Robin. *My Loin Cloth Has No Pockets*.
Produced by Don Richmond, Howlin' Dog Records.
2007, compact disc.

Various Artists. *Songs for Junior Rangers*. Produced
by the National Park Service. 2012, compact disc. All
songs by Jeff Wolin, except Junior Ranger by Krishel
Augustine, Tribe Navajo.

Elliot, Doug. *Bullfrogs On Your Mind: Stories, Songs,
Adventures from the Swamps to the Henhouse*.
Native Ground Music. 1997, compact disc.

———*Crawdads, Doodlebugs & Creasy Greens:
Songs, Stories & Lore Celebrating the Natural World*.
Native Ground Music. 1996, compact disc.

STORES

The Recycled Lamb
2081 Youngfield Street
Golden, CO 80401
www.recycledlamb.com

Ontario Knife Company
P.O. Box 145
Franklinville, NY 14737
www.ontarioknife.com

Moscow Hide and Fur
P.O. Box 8918
Moscow, ID 83843
www.hideandfur.com

Sun Oven International
www.sunoven.com

OUTDOOR IMMERSION PROGRAMS

Four Corners School of Outdoor Education
Janet Ross, Executive Director
49 West 600 South
Monticello, UT 84535
www.fourcornersschool.org

Cottonwood Institute
P.O. Box 7067
Denver, CO 80207
www.cottonwoodinstitute.org

Earth Knack
Robin Blankenship, Owner
3907 Lovers Way
Crestone, CO 81131
www.earthknack.com

**The Wayfaring Band: Special Needs Populations
Outdoor and Travel Programming**
Andrea Moore, Executive Director
3327 Brighton Blvd
Denver, CO 80216
www.thewayfaringband.com

ROBIN BLANKENSHIP, owner of the Earth Knack
School, has been teaching primitive skills, sustainable modern
life skill courses, and leading wilderness treks since 1978.
She has three adult children and lives in Crestone, Colorado.
Robin is also the author of *Earth Knack: Stone Age Skills for
the 21st Century.*